*The* MONOCLE
*Travel Guide Series*

# Amsterdam

For more information,
please visit *gestalten.com*

———

Bibliographic information
published by the Deutsche
Nationalbibliothek: The
Deutsche Nationalbibliothek lists
this publication in the Deutsche
Nationalbibliografie; detailed
bibliographic data are available
online at *dnb.d-nb.de*

Monocle editor in chief
and chairman: *Tyler Brûlé*
Monocle editor: *Andrew Tuck*
Books editor: *Joe Pickard*
Guide editor: *Mikaela Aitken*

———

Designed by *Monocle*
Proofreading by *Monocle*
Typeset in *Plantin & Helvetica*

———

Printed by *Offsetdruckerei
Grammlich, Pliezhausen*

Made in Germany

Published by *Gestalten*, Berlin 2017
ISBN 978-3-89955-905-7

© Die Gestalten Verlag GmbH &
Co. KG, Berlin 2017

This book was printed on
paper certified by the FSC®

# Welcome
—— Alluring
Amsterdam

Boats bobbing on canals, rows of colourful houses, cosy pubs and friendly locals: it's easy to be swayed by the patent charms of the *Dutch capital*. But dwell a little longer and you'll see that the city's appeal runs much deeper.

The compact centre is a medley of heritage-listed buildings, independent retail and a growing collection of *top tables*. Just a 10-minute cycle further out (most places are a 10-minute cycle away here) will land you in vibrant, evolving neighbourhoods that meld bold contemporary architecture with socially conscious *Amsterdam School* housing developments. Sprawling green spaces pop with colour when the *tulips bloom* in spring. And across the city there's a compelling cultural offering, including a hefty hoard of works by the *Dutch masters*, art deco cinemas and post-industrial lots repurposed for *gigs and exhibitions.*

But like all cities, Amsterdam has its shortfalls. It has a reputation for loutish tourists and some argue that its famed *tradition of liberalism* is losing steam due to the rise in populism. However, the local government is working hard to mend these faults and position the city as a *haven for business* by making the most of its highly educated English-speaking population and low corporate taxes.

Amsterdam continues to build on its reputation as a *dynamic and welcoming* place. So turn the page and join us on a journey through the cobbled streets and smooth snaking bikeways of this wonderful city. — (M)

# Contents
—— Navigating the city

Use the key below to help navigate the guide section by section.

 Hotels

 Food and drink

 Retail

 Things we'd buy

 Essays

 Culture

 Design and architecture

 Sport and fitness

 Walks

# Map
## —— Lay of the land and sea

The Netherlands shouldn't exist: more than a quarter of the country lies beneath sea level, including its capital (the parliament may sit in The Hague but this is the capital city). Yet by the 13th century, fishermen based themselves on the peat swamps near the Amstel river and built a dam, giving rise to Amsterdam.

In the Middle Ages the series of dykes and dams expanded, creating pieces of low-lying land reclaimed from the sea and allowing Amsterdam to expand into a small port town. Trade boomed in the 16th and 17th centuries and the subsequent wealth saw the network of canals and houses more than double.

The industrial revolution saw the addition of a west entrance to the harbour and another belt of land, including the three islands that house Centraal station. Today town-planners are looking to the harbour to develop dynamic neighbourhoods in the Noord and Eastern Docklands, while Zuidas in the south is bolstering its role as the central business district.

Kraanspoor

NOORD

Nieuwendammerdijk Harbour

WH Vliegenbos

Eye Filmmuseum

IJ

• Centraal station

Muziekgebouw aan 't IJ & Bimhuis

Museum Ons' Lieve
Heer op Solder

Nemo Science Museum

EASTERN DOCKLANDS

De Oude Kerk

• Het Scheepvaartmuseum
• Architectuurcentrum Amsterdam (Arcam)

CENTRUM

Funenpark

Hortus
Botanicus
Amsterdam

De Gooyer Windmill

Artis Royal Zoo

• De Bazel

DE PLANTAGE

Steigereiland

Magere Brug

Oosterpark

OOST

DE PIJP

Amstel

Sarphatipark

0          500M          N

# Need to know
—— Defining the Dutch

Amsterdam is considered to be one of the most liberal cities in the world but there are a few nuances to wrap your head around before arriving. From kissing three times to ordering the right-sized beer, here are a few handy tips and fast facts to help you blend in with the locals.

### Greetings
Meet and greet

When in a business setting or meeting someone for the first time, a firm handshake will suffice. If you're meeting a friend, a trio of kisses is the go-to greeting. In general the Dutch don't beat around the bush but don't mistake this directness for poor manners. Quite the contrary: a polite demeanour is very much appreciated. Finally, when it comes to attending a birthday party, be sure to congratulate all of the family members on the anniversary as well – and they will likely congratulate you right back.

### Urban planning
Building a case

There's little room for new development in the Unesco World Heritage-listed 17th-century canal ring that circles the city centre. As such, town-planners are working to solve the housing shortage by attracting residential developments to post-industrial areas through urban-renewal projects and commissioning attractive contemporary public buildings. To see this change in action venture out from the centre and visit the Eye Filmmuseum in Noord, the Westergasfabriek in Westerpark and Bimhuis in the Eastern Docklands. Also keep an eye on the central business district of Zuidas, which has become a favoured base for international headquarters.

*Hold on folks, we're turning right!*

### Cycling
Pedal to the metal

With the canal's one-way street system, driving can be a frustrating experience – so cycling is by far the best way to get around. Remember to indicate your direction by sticking out a hand and bear in mind that traffic from the right has right of way. Helmets aren't compulsory but lights at night are. Also be sure to pedal hard: if an Amsterdammer spots you dallying in the bike lane you'll likely cop an earful.

### Liberal values
The new normal

We all think of Amsterdam as a liberal city but its liberal policies may have more to do with pragmatism than tolerance. To the Dutch, choosing to turn a blind eye to cannabis and decriminalising prostitution is sensible: it removes the lure of vice and repositions it as mundane. However, the city is still trying to find such a balance with the rowdy stag and hen dos. And take note: a coffeeshop is not for caffeine.

## Money
### Cash in hand

Maestro is king in the city and the card machines used by retailers and smaller cafés don't always accept Visa or Amex. To avoid an awkward conversation about what will be left as collateral while you dash to the nearest ATM, be sure to carry a little extra cash. Tipping isn't customary but if you do happen to experience excellent service – it's surprisingly sporadic in the capital – then 10 per cent is recommended.

## Beer
### Raise a glass

Amsterdam is the birthplace of some of the world's most famous beer brands. Ask for *een biertje* (a beer) in a pub and you'll be given the house lager on tap, often Amstel or Heineken. The typical Dutch beer glass is a half pint – ordering a full pint is a faux pas – and should be topped with about 2cm of foam. This foam is part of the beer experience; locals call foamless beer "dead beer". Ask for an *amsterdammertje* if you want your beer served in a traditional Dutch glass.

*The best solution to any problem – a healing draft of lager*

*Now that boat looks like a nice place to perch*

## Language
### Dutch masters

Most Dutch speak at least two languages and they're among the best non-native English speakers in the world. Children start learning English from the age of 10 and then take on at least one other foreign language in high school (often German, French or Spanish). This, alongside the low barriers to entry, is what attracts so much foreign investment to the city. Plus, all English TV shows and films are subtitled rather than dubbed, making a trip to the cinema a breeze.

## Why 'IJ' is not a typo
### Learning the lingo

When it comes to English speakers learning the Dutch language, you'll notice that many words – such as colours, vegetables and fruits – have Germanic roots. Reading proves slightly easier than interpreting the guttural speech. One important nuance to note is the use of "IJ" as a single letter. It's pronounced along the lines of "aey" and is derived from a word that means water. It's also the official name given to the harbour and river.

## Terrace culture
### Alfresco drinking

As soon as there's the slightest hint of spring in the air Amsterdammers spill out onto the terraces of cafés and restaurants. The Dutch even have a special saying for this affinity with perching outdoors: *een terrasje pakken*. This translates as "take a terrace" but it's commonly used as a verb to suggest to friends or colleagues that you grab a drink outside. Fitting for a city with picturesque canals and parks aplenty.

## Food and drink
### Wine and dine

The Dutch have peculiar food preferences. They like their bread with all sorts of spreads and sprinkles and enjoy starchy meals such as *hutspot* (potatoes, carrots and onions) and *andijviestamppot* (potatoes and endive), as well as fried snacks that are sometimes dispensed from vending machines (*see page 32*). If you're craving a meal at one of the city's top tables be sure to call ahead because most are rammed night after night. Peak time is between 18.30 and 19.30 and kitchens close relatively early.

*Why editors have a problem with waffle is beyond me*

# Hotels
── Where to stay

The hotel selection in Amsterdam is as much a journey into the architectural ethos of the city as it is an offering of accommodation. You'll find modern and towering chains if that's what you're hankering after (Hotel Okura fits the bill) but don't overlook Amsterdam's more unique options. In keeping with the most intriguing buildings around the city, these hotels take advantage of existing structures in pragmatic but respectful fashion. There are hotels that consist of more than 20 buildings tethered together, that occupy the repurposed sites of music schools, juvenile detention centres and newspaper offices, or that simply enjoy architecture dating back to the 17th century.

Also worth a look is the new wave of design hotels that skew towards a younger clientele, with more affordable rooms and creative concepts. Check in and check them out.

① Hotel V Fizeaustraat, Watergraafsmeer
*The 1970s with a twist*

The Fizeaustraat branch, which opened in 2017, is Hotel V's third location in the capital. It's a little further afield, in the east's developing district of Watergraafsmeer, but it's only a 10-minute taxi ride from the canal ring and in our opinion the standout of the trio.

In-house designer Mirjam Espinosa has seamlessly blended a modish 1970s aesthetic into the boxy Piet Zanstra building and carefully chosen furnishings that echo the surrounding greenery. All 91 rooms are finished with hexagonal solid-oak parquet floors, pebble-grey linens and woollen tapestries. The ever-friendly staff are on hand 24/7 to assist with any requests, including bike rental, international newspapers, laundry and in-room massages.
*2 Fizeaustraat, 1097 SC*
*+31 (0)20 662 3233*
*hotelvfizeaustraat.nl*

MONOCLE COMMENT: The hotel may feel like it's out in the sticks but that doesn't deter Amsterdammers from dining in Jeroen van Spall's always-teeming restaurant, The Lobby. The house special is *flammkuche* ("flame cake") from the Alsace region.

**②**

## Pulitzer Hotel, Centrum
*Room for variety*

Peter Pulitzer's hotel first opened in 1970 in the retail district of De 9 Straatjes and, after extensive renovations, reopened in 2016. The canal-side space spans 25 connected 17th and 18th-century townhouses with 225 rooms, 19 of them suites.

No two rooms are the same: architect and creative director Jacu Strauss stayed in each and every one to mull over the fit-out. "We chose a range of styles and finishes that suit the buildings' 400 years of history," he says. The result is an eclectic mix, with velvet-upholstered armchairs sitting alongside modern desks. One thing is consistent: each room has its own marble bathroom.
*315-331 Prinsengracht, 1016 GZ*
*+31 (0)20 523 5235*
*pulitzeramsterdam.com*

MONOCLE COMMENT: It's hard to beat the extra space and canal-side views in the suites. A handful offer guests a private entrance and can be booked upon request.

*I suppose there are worse places to get lost*

③
Morgan & Mees, Westerpark
*Lesson in luxury*

This petite hotel may sit on the corner of two congested streets but its nine rooms are relaxed, good-looking and, most importantly, welcoming. The former 17th-century school was transformed by hospitality entrepreneurs Myrthe Slotemaker and Roger Peetoom, along with designer Marius Haverkamp in 2014. Peetoom's wife, Anne Claus, led the interior design, choosing parqueted wooden floors, mid-century chairs and modern artwork to decorate the rooms.

When booking it's worth opting for the single-storey rooms as the sleeping arrangements in the duplexes are slightly more cramped. The bar and restaurant on the ground floor offer room service or, if the weather's good, head to the terrace at the front.
*2-6 Tweede Hugo de Grootstraat, 1052 LC*
*+31 (0)20 233 4930*
*morganandmees.com*

MONOCLE COMMENT: The boutique nature of the hotel lends itself well to slightly longer stints in the city. The downside is that there's no gym or spa but it's in a prime spot for a jog around the canal ring instead (*see page 127*).

④
The Hoxton, Centrum
*Mid-century marvel*

The Hoxton is another newcomer to the host of design hotels in De 9 Straatjes, having opened its doors in 2015. Inconspicuous from the street, the 111 rooms sit within five interjoining canal houses, one of which was the residence of the city's mayor in the 17th century (two more classically designed concept rooms are in this section of the building and can be booked upon request).

Each room is different but the reupholstered vintage furniture and exposed copper pipes in the bathrooms neatly tie the hotel's cosy mid-century theme together. If you're after a quick start to the day, hang your breakfast bag outside your door in the evening to have complimentary yoghurt, granola, banana and fresh orange juice waiting for you in the morning.
*255 Herengracht, 1016 BJ*
*+31 (0)20 888 5555*
*thehoxton.com*

MONOCLE COMMENT: The restaurant and bar, Lotti's, is run by Soho House, meaning the breakfast menu is tip-top and the cocktails are stirred extra-strong. It also cleverly conceals the reception desk, which is hiding beneath the stairs on the right.

*Sleep well*
——
Orthosomatic mattresses feature in all rooms

2
212–231

**5**

Conservatorium Hotel, Oud-Zuid
*Light touch*

This neo-gothic building designed by Dutch architect Daniel Knuttel began life as a bank in 1897 and a century later was home to the Conservatorium van Amsterdam. When the music school outgrew it, the Set Hotels group bought the space and transformed it into a 129-room hotel.

Italian designer and architect Piero Lissoni has reinvigorated the historic building, with natural light playing a key part. The lobby and brasserie sit beneath a glass atrium, while many rooms benefit from the heritage-listed windows. Its closest neighbours are the city's most celebrated museums including the Rijksmuseum, the Stedelijk and Van Gogh, as well as the lesser-known but still very much worthwhile Moco Museum.
*27 Van Baerlestraat, 1071 AN*
*+31 (0)20 570 0000*
*conservatoriumhotel.com*

MONOCLE COMMENT: Not only is there a gym (*see page 124*), a gin bar and a top restaurant led by Schilo Van Coevorden but also a luxury shopping gallery. Shops include Bentley (also the hotel's car of choice for airport transfers), Bonebakker jewellers, Skins Cosmetics and Meraki hair salon.

### Shop and stay
—

Amsterdam-based design company Droog has set up a one-bedroom hotel on the top floor of its shop (*see page 49*) and studio in Centrum. The space, which also includes a long, light-filled living area, is available to hire for small events as well.
*droog.com*

Maison Rika, Centrum
*Boutique hideaway*

In the heart of the De 9 Straatjes neighbourhood, one of the traditional 200-year-old corner houses has been converted into a pocket-sized guesthouse. Previously serving as a gallery, the space was acquired by Swedish fashion designer and former interior decorator Ulrika Lundgren in the hope of creating a cosy pied-à-terre. "People who come here don't want flashy five-star hotels: they're looking for something unique, something secret," she says.

Maison Rika only has two rooms, each of which occupies an entire floor and offers guests a panoramic view of the Herengracht canal. The house's ground floor delivers its fair share of distraction too: it simultaneously serves as a lobby, a concept boutique (*see page 52*) and a pop-up gallery. Although breakfast isn't included in the price, regular refreshments and a selection of small but tasty snacks are brought to the room during the day.
*12 Oude Spiegelstraat, 1016 BM*
*+31 (0)20 330 1112*
*rikastudios.com*

MONOCLE COMMENT: The free-of-charge concierge service will help you secure those hard-to-get restaurant reservations as well as tickets to the hottest shows. Guests can also pick up a copy of the in-house biannual publication *Rika Magazine*, with striking fashion pictorials and punchy articles.

⑦
Hotel Okura, De Pijp
*Tall storeys*

Hotel Okura is an odd sight to behold: a 23-storey tower bordering the low-rise residential neighbourhood of De Pijp. The Japanese chain's only European outpost was designed by Dutch architect Bernard Bijvoet and opened in 1971.

A 10-minute cycle from the canal ring and an eight-minute taxi from the commercial district, it's well positioned for those in town on business. The 300 rooms are comfortable and decorated with dark-wood panelling and Japanese-inspired decor. Guests also have access to a lap pool, gym and sauna.

*333 Ferdinand Bolstraat, 1072 LH*
*+31 (0)20 678 7111*
*okura.nl*

MONOCLE COMMENT: Yamazato, the Michelin-starred restaurant on the ground floor, is one of Hotel Okura's four dining spots. Executive chef Masanori Tomikawa started as a porter in the hotel's Tokyo outpost before moving to Amsterdam to work in the kitchens in 1984. After training under Akira Oshima, Tomikawa took the reins. His *kaiseki* menu (a traditional Japanese multi-course affair) will impress any client.

### Design hotels

A spate of new design hotels has shaken up the scene, targeting younger audiences with creative concepts and more affordable prices.

01 **Volkshotel, Oost:** This 172-room hotel opened in 2014 in the former offices of Dutch daily newspaper *De Volkskrant*. Evidence of this past life can be seen throughout the design, including photos from the city's counterculture.
*volkshotel.nl*

02 **Zoku, De Plantage:** This is more suited to young professionals who are either moving to the city or in town for a slightly longer period; its services include business-registration assistance and access to office equipment. The bar offers meeting rooms, co-working spaces and a fine wine menu.
*livezoku.com*

03 **Pension Homeland, Eastern Docklands:** The proximity to the harbour and various museums is the drawcard but the 1960s and 1970s-inspired interiors may be a little loud for some.
*pensionhomeland.com*

*It's time for some dogged exploration*

⑧
Lloyd Hotel & Cultural Embassy,
Eastern Docklands
*Come one, come all*

It's a rather peculiar approach
for a hotel to cater to all budgets
under one roof but that's been
Lloyd Hotel's concept since
opening in 2004. "We wanted
people to fit in and to be able to
order breakfast in bed whether
they were a one-star or five-star
guest," says co-founder and
artistic director Suzanne Oxenaar.

In its 100-year history the
storied building, which is located
in the old Eastern Docklands, has
served as both a refugee and
juvenile-detention centre, as well as
an artists' studio. Top Dutch design
talent such as MVRDV and Joep Van
Lieshout worked to transform the
existing spaces to accommodate
117 contemporary rooms, an
expansive restaurant, a library
and exhibition spaces for the
in-house Cultural Embassy.
*34 Oostelijke Handelskade, 1019 BN*
*+31 (0)20 561 3607*
*lloydhotel.com*

MONOCLE COMMENT: Hotel
guests are afforded free entry
to the Cultural Embassy's busy
calendar of events, which includes
philosophy talks, modern-art
exhibitions and annual Japanese
market MonoJapan.

⑨
The Dylan, Centrum
*Heritage hospitality*

The Dylan is a dependable place
to hang your hat while in town.
Located on the canal ring in De
9 Straatjes, the five interjoining
buildings operated as a charity
from the 18th century; the original
baker's ovens from the food bank
line the walls of in-house French
restaurant Vinkeles.

The privately owned hotel
has 40 rooms, 16 of which were
refurbished in 2014 by Dutch
designer Remy Meijers. Our
preference rests with the Scandi-
simplicity of the five loft suites.
Just watch your step as you weave
between buildings: a condition of
its heritage status means there are
a few sudden floor changes.
*384 Keizersgracht, 1016 GB*
*+31 (0)20 530 2010*
*dylanamsterdam.com*

MONOCLE COMMENT: While the
linens may be Italian, the plump
beds are Dutch. Nilson mattresses
will ensure a restful night's sleep.

⑩
## W Hotel, Centrum
*Bank on it*

Two sister buildings just off Dam Square mark W Hotel's first foray onto the Dutch hotel scene. The luxury chain planned to open one 172-room hotel in the 1903 modernist telephone exchange building but a happy accident saw owner Liran Wizman also acquire the old Kas Bank across the street.

While the handsome exteriors of the Exchange might seem more alluring, the stately feel of the Bank's interior has clear appeal. Its centrepiece is The Duchess restaurant in the original banking hall, with hand-painted floor tiles, ornate wooden door frames and a sweeping stained-glass roof. Of the Bank's 66 rooms, 10 are spacious suites. Furry friends are also welcomed – and even catered for on the room-service menus.
*175 Spuistraat, 1012 VN*
*+31 (0)20 811 2500*
*wamsterdam.com*

MONOCLE COMMENT: The benefits of neighbouring buildings is the roster of amenities available to all guests. On the Exchange side is a rooftop bar, plunge pool and steak restaurant, while on the Bank side is a gym, concept store (*see pages 46 to 47*) and day spa hidden behind a four-tonne vault door.

### Grand Hotel Amrâth

On the border of Centrum and the Eastern Docklands, not too far from Centraal station, is the gargantuan brick Grand Hotel Amrâth. Heavily influenced by art nouveau, it's an early example of Amsterdam School; architect Johan van der Mey was commissioned by six shipping companies in 1912 to design a shared office building. Its close proximity to the docks allowed the companies to sell tickets for voyages to the likes of the Dutch East Indies.

Van der Mey wove nautical motifs into the stained glass, stonework, furniture and finishings; the exterior features a gallery of stone heads. It opened as a five-star hotel in 2007 but the rooms are a tad garish. The common areas are open to the public.
*amrathamsterdam.com*

# Food and drink
—— Going Dutch

Although the Dutch are known worldwide for their cheese, pancakes and apple pie, Amsterdam is not famed as a culinary destination. But if you know where to look, there's plenty going on in the city of canals.

Recent years have seen a huge shift from the exotic to the homegrown, with nearly all of the best restaurants now focusing on using seasonal, local ingredients from sustainable producers. This means menus that change regularly, inventive vegetarian cuisine despite the country's traditional obsession with meat, and modern Dutch fare that reinvents the old classics.

Very few locals live in the centre of Amsterdam so the best places are often a bit further afield. Amsterdammers love to eat out so hop on your bike and join them – but best to book ahead.

① Buffet van Odette, Centrum
*Bistro style*

Odette Rigterink has had a clear vision ever since she started cooking food and selling it at a market in 1994: good meals made with good products, to be savoured and enjoyed. These days Buffet van Odette is a local institution famous for its truffle-cheese omelette, Frank's Smokehouse smoked salmon and sticky-toffee cake.

Its French-bistro style makes it perfect for a long, relaxed lunch accompanied by natural wine but you can also pop in for breakfast or call ahead to try the seasonal harissa mussels at dinner.
*598 Prinsengracht, 1017 KS*
*+31 (0)20 423 6034*
*buffet-amsterdam.nl*

**② Bar Spek, De Baarsjes**
*Leisurely lunches*

Opening in time for breakfast and closing well after midnight, Bar Spek wants people to stay all day, making it a favourite among the young, freelance crowd in this increasingly vibrant part of town.

It's a low-key neighbourhood spot with an enormous menu that covers everything from overnight oats and eggs to pulled pork focaccia and truffle pizza – plus it's sat right on a canal, making it fantastic in summer. Drop by for a lazy lunch or check out the website for details of events, such as the popular gin-and-tonic nights.
*1 Admiraal de Ruijterweg, 1057 JT*
*+31 (0)20 618 8102*
*barspek.nl*

**③ Guts & Glory, Centrum**
*Globetrotting cuisine*

You know you're onto something unique when you enter Guts & Glory through its unusual exterior. Dutch chefs and best friends Guillaume de Beer and Freek van Noortwijk opened the restaurant with the idea of using every part of the animal, rotating the menu every three months.

The duo have now moved on to country-specific cuisines and the interior is always decorated to match. For all its fame this is an easygoing place, perfect for dinner with friends. Call a week ahead for weekend bookings.
*6 Utrechtsestraat, 1017 VN*
*+31 (0)20 362 0030*
*gutsglory.nl*

**4**
Worst Wijncafé, Westelijke Eilanden
*Nice sausage*

In a quiet part of town, this haunt was set up as a way for owner Kees Elfring (*pictured*) to bring quality sausage to the city, something he felt was lacking. Amsterdammers clearly agreed with him because the place is full every night with people trying out the homemade selection, such as the wild boar, the fennel and the lobster.

The starter-sized servings are ideal for sharing during a *borrel* (evening drink) with friends. The pigs' trotters – one of the few imported ingredients – are highly recommended.
*171 Barentszstraat, 1013 NM*
*+31 (0)20 625 6167*
*deworst.nl*

**5**
Betty's, Rijnbuurt
*Home comforts*

Stepping into Betty's is a bit like stepping into owners Gido and Caroline Schweitzer's living room. This homely vegetarian restaurant has been a two-person operation ever since it opened in 1988, allowing the Schweitzers to create a place where diners can stay all night if they choose.

The three-course menu changes every few weeks but one thing you can expect is inventive food packed with flavour that contains influences from all over the world. Betty's is an institution with a big heart. Reservations are essential.
*75 Rijnstraat, 1079 GX*
*+31 (0)20 644 5896*
*bettys.nl*

### 6
**Spang Makandra, De Pijp**
*Spice sensation*

This tiny restaurant is always busy – and with good reason. The decor isn't particularly inspiring but the food is arguably the best Surinamese-Javanese food you can get in Amsterdam. Spang Makandra opened its doors in 1978 and remains a family business to this day. It is now run by son Budi Moestadja, who is usually on hand to provide recommendations.

It's a relaxed place and more often than not packed with regulars enjoying generous portions of roti with *pom* (a chicken and root-vegetable dish). Pop by for lunch and order the house special for a culinary tour through the former Dutch empire, comprising fried rice, noodles, chicken satay and Javanese *frikandel*, topped with a fried egg and a super-spicy potato sambal.
*39 Gerard Doustraat, 1072 VK*
*+31 (0)20 670 5081*
*spangmakandra.nl*

High steaks
The owners also run De Nachtwacht grillhouse

**Potato pleasure**

*Vlaamse patat* (Flemish-style chips) are almost a deity in the Netherlands. Hole-in-the-wall Vlaams Friteshuis Vleminckx has been serving golden cones of *patat* since 1957. For something different, try the satay sauce or *patatje oorlog*. *vleminckxdesausmeester.nl*

### 7
Venus & Adonis, Jordaan
*Rare discovery*

If you're on the hunt for a juicy steak with some grilled tiger prawns, flawlessly seared scallops or, perhaps, a serving of lobster tail, look no further than Venus & Adonis. The meat is exclusively sourced from Dutch female Blonde d'Aquitaine cows for a more tasty and tender steak, and the restaurant makes good use of its charcoal grill.

The eclectic interior – think hexagonal hanging lights, yellow-suede chairs and a wooden ceiling – creates a comfortable and sophisticated ambiance.
*274 Prinsengracht, 1016 HH*
*+31 (0)20 421 1848*
*venusenadonis.nl*

(8)

## Little Collins, De Pijp
*Best of the brunch*

Run by an Australian-Dutch couple, Little Collins channels that sunny Melbourne feeling with friendly staff and global flavours and influences. It gets busy at weekends (the only time it doesn't take reservations) so go during the week if possible.

The restaurant takes the now ubiquitous avo on toast to new levels with fennel, goat's cheese and dukkah; it also serves delicious waffles with English bacon or kimchi pancakes. In summer the outdoor terrace makes this place hard to beat.

*19F Eerste Sweelinckstraat, 1073 CL*
*+31 (0)20 753 9636*
*littlecollins.nl*

(9)

Scheepskameel, Eastern Docklands
*Unfussy fine dining*

The Scheepskameel experience begins with maître d' Bob, who greets you at the door like an old friend. "It should feel like coming home to your family," says head chef Tijs Jeurissen (*pictured*).

With its high ceilings and naval history, Scheepskameel (Ship's Camel) is not homely but it works. The dinner-only à la carte menu is European cooking that is suitable for all budgets and attracts a diverse clientele. Leave room: the madeleines are famously good.

*Gebouw 24, 7 Kattenburgerstraat, 1018 JA*
*+31 (0)20 337 9680*
*scheepskameel.nl*

(10)
New Werktheater,
Eastern Docklands
*Daring dining*

Design agency Staat breathed
new life into this 1970s theatre by
transforming it into "a space for
everything we love", says creative
director Merel Korteweg. Though
grey on the outside, the interior is
anything but. Alongside a photo
studio and co-working space
you'll find a restaurant that drags
sleepy Amsterdammers out of bed
with hearty European breakfasts
– or pop in at lunchtime for
adventurous plates such as venison
croquettes. Eat dinner elsewhere:
the restaurant closes at 19.00.
*75 Oostenburgergracht, 1018 NC*
*+31 (0)20 572 1385*
*newwerktheater.com*

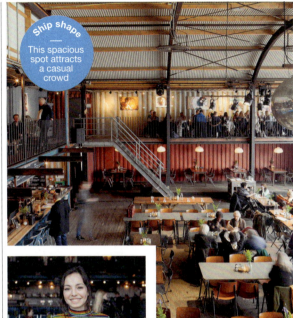

*Ship shape*
—
This spacious
spot attracts
a casual
crowd

(11)
Pllek, Noord
*Take me to the river*

For a taste of the grittier north
take the free city ferry to this
restaurant-café constructed from
shipping containers on PllekBeach
along the IJ river. Grab a seat at the
shared tables and enjoy seasonal
fare such as mushrooms, steamed
mackerel or falafel.
    In summer this is a popular
place to soak up sunshine on the
deckchairs but its spacious interior
is also inviting in colder weather. It
hosts film screenings, yoga sessions
and music performances year-
round and is a family-friendly spot
that attracts a laidback crowd.
*59 Tt. Neveritaweg, 1033 WB*
*+31 (0)20 290 0020*
*pllek.nl*

**Must-try**
**Haring from Nico Kras**
This delicacy of raw, salted
herring is best enjoyed in
a *broodje* (bread bun) with
crunchy onions and sweet
pickles at Nico Kras. The
herring here is from the
coveted catch known as
*Hollandse nieuwe.*
+31 (0)20 622 0767

**12**

## La Perla, Jordaan
*Pizza perfection*

Founded in Jordaan's charming
"Little Italy" street, La Perla is a
small corner restaurant that draws
a mighty crowd. Most come for the
pizza, which is packed with flavour,
perfectly cooked and pleasingly
irregular in shape. The menu only
offers 11 types, with variations
on the themes of cheese and pork
featuring heavily.

Buffalo mozzarella is delivered
fresh from Italy and everything
is cooked in the wood-fuelled
brick oven, making this one of the
best pizza restaurants in the city.
Takeaway is also available.
*53 Tweede Tuindwarsstraat, 1015 RZ*
*+31 (0)20 624 8828*
*pizzaperla.nl*

**13**

## Wolf Atelier, Westelijke Eilanden
*Rising above it all*

Chef Michael Wolf's restaurant is
the sort of place you go to impress
someone – or treat yourself. The
structure itself is striking: a mostly
glass building that perches over
the water on a 1920s industrial
railway bridge. Upon entering the
sleek grey-and-brass dining room
you'll receive a welcome box with
a mint, refreshing towel and bottle
of filtered water. Lunchtime diners
can enjoy six tartares in three
sizes, while dinner is an inventive
European menu of meat and fish.
Try the 15-course tasting menu for
a journey through Wolf's kitchen.
*20 Westerdoksplein, 1013 AZ*
*+31 (0)20 344 6428*
*wolfatelier.nl*

### Fast and fried

Pronounced "fay-bo" and
named after Ferdinand
Bolstraat, the street where the
chef learned his trade, Febo is a
fast-food chain where you can
get fried snacks from a vending
machine. Popular choices
include the *kipcorn* chicken
stick and *frikadel* sausage.
*febo.nl*

### 14
Bak, Westelijke Eilanden
*Room with a view*

Despite beginning life as a pop-up, Bak has become a much-celebrated mainstay since opening in 2012. Its menu centres around top-quality regional produce and the chefs only use meat and fish caught in the wild. With at least 500 natural wines available, including the increasingly popular orange variety, it may well have one of the largest collections in the country.

Situated in a former warehouse, the whitewashed room enables diners to enjoy the view across the old harbour and the IJ river in an elegant setting.
*408 Van Diemenstraat, 1013 CR*
*+31 (0)20 737 2553*
*bakrestaurant.nl*

### 15
Sama Sebo, Oud-Zuid
*Indonesian feast*

When Daniel Woldringh opened Sama Sebo in 1969 he had no idea that his restaurant would become a cornerstone of Amsterdam's popular Indonesian food scene. Decades later the 1970s interior still charms, with copper pots and pans hanging from the low ceiling and a wooden bar to perch at.

The main event is the *rijsttafel* (rice table), a spectacular spread of more than 20 small sharing dishes such as beef rendang, chicken satay and tiger prawns.
*27 Pieter Cornelisz Hooftstraat, 1071 BL.*
*+31 (0)20 662 8146*
*samasebo.nl*

### 16
Mook Pancakes, Oud-West
*Go flat out*

Pancakes may be a national dish but Mook isn't doing things the traditional way. Opened in 2016 by entrepreneurs Sten van den Bedem and Sammy Salimian as an experiment in healthy US-style pancakes, it has become a much-loved gem.

Made with spelt flour, buttermilk and eggs (vegan options are also available), these thick, fluffy delights are served three-in-a-pile with anything from bacon and maple syrup to peanut butter and fruit. Throw in juice and sofas and this becomes an infallible brunch spot.
*34 De Clercqstraat, 1052 MZ*
*+31 (0)20 334 6995*

*Sharing dishes? I'm not familiar with that concept*

18

De Japanner, De Pijp
*Late-night bites*

Modelled on a Japanese *izakaya* (gastropub for after-work drinks), De Japanner hits the sweet spot between restaurant and bar. The small menu features Japanese dishes with local seafood, such as herring sashimi, and *izakaya* classics such as *agedashidofu* (deep-fried tofu), all perfect for washing down with Japanese whiskey, saké or even a bottle of Tokyo craft beer.

It's walk-in only from 19.00, giving the place an informal feel. Plus, unusually for Amsterdam, the kitchen doesn't close until the front door does; 03.00 at the weekend.
*228 Albert Cuypstraat, 1073 BN*
*+31 (0)20 233 9939*
*dejapanner.com*

17

Festina Lente, Jordaan
*Canal-side lunch spot*

Beloved by locals, this living room-style café is all about taking a second to catch your breath in an increasingly hectic world. A café has been here in one form or another for more than a century and this iteration has been popular for lunch breaks and post-work drinks ever since it opened in 1998.

Think healthy and inexpensive soups, salads and sandwiches in a homely wooden interior complete with squishy sofas and shelves of books. Come summer, grab a table outside on the pretty Looiersgracht and watch canal life pass by.
*40B Looiersgracht, 1016 VS*
*+31 (0)20 638 1412*
*cafefestinalente.nl*

19

D'Vijff Vlieghen, Centrum
*Culinary museum*

Although D'Vijff Vlieghen (Five Flies) opened its doors in 1939, the dazzling interior – with its antique glassware, tiles, prints and wooden beams – feels centuries older. Five rooms provide plenty of snug spots that belie the restaurant's size (270 covers excluding the private areas).

Ask for a tour if it's quiet to see the Rembrandt etchings and Walt Disney drawing in the guestbook. The menu is modern Dutch, featuring the likes of tuna steak baked in *speculaas* spices and ice cream with herbs.
*294-302 Spuistraat, 1012 VX*
*+31 (0)20 530 4060*
*vijffvlieghen.nl*

## ⑳ John Dory, Centrum
*Catch of the day*

John Dory is all about regional seafood prepared in exciting ways. The restaurant is spread across two floors of a 17th-century former canal-side warehouse: there's a small bar for oysters and wine downstairs and a more formal fish restaurant upstairs.

Lights suspended from fishing rope and wooden beams make this a cosy dinner spot for those seeking a taste of old-world Amsterdam. The menu changes daily according to the catch from the North Sea but don't miss the red mullet if it's available – it's the owner's favourite.
*999 Prinsengracht, 1017 KM*
*+31 (0)20 622 9044*
*johndory.nl*

## ㉑ De Kas, Watergraafsmeer
*Garden party*

It doesn't get any fresher than eating food grown in a restaurant's own garden. Located in the stately Frankendael Park, De Kas and its nursery occupy old municipal greenhouses renovated by Dutch designer Piet Boon (restaurants in greenhouses are somewhat of a trend in the city, perhaps in an attempt to maximise light during the moody winter months).

The uncomplicated, vegetable-oriented menu changes daily depending on what's harvested and includes meat, fish and dairy products.
*3 Kamerlingh Onneslaan, 1097 DE*
*+31 (0)20 462 4562*
*restaurantdekas.nl*

### 22
### Choux, Centrum
*Conversation starter*

You'd be hard pressed to guess
that Choux's smart address inside
Spring House – a multidisciplinary
space for creatives – used to be the
site of a distillery on a street known
for prostitution and depravity.
These days the restaurant attracts
a different professional crowd.

Owners Figo van Onna and
Merijn van Berlo experiment
with umami-loaded sustainable
ingredients such as seaweed to get
people thinking about meat-free
cooking. The results are impressive,
particularly when enjoyed with a
specially paired glass of natural wine.
*128 De Ruijterkade, 1011 AC*
*+31 (0)61 651 2364*
*choux.nl*

### 23
### Wilde Zwijnen, Indische Buurt
*Far from a boar*

Wilde Zwijnen was one of the first
upmarket restaurants to open in
up-and-coming Indische Buurt
back in 2010 and its modern take
on Dutch food has helped draw
interest to the area. Expect regional
vegetables prepared in inventive
ways alongside fresh seafood and
make sure you try the eponymous
wild boar if available.

The restaurant has an intimate
feel, even if it's full. For a more
speedy meal drop into the
adjoining Eetcafé and feast on
tapas-inspired bites such as cod
chips and aubergine cream.
*23 Javaplein, 1095 CJ*
*+31 (0)20 463 3043*
*wildezwijnen.com*

The holes
mean that the
cheese has fewer
calories, right?

**㉔**
Vuurtoreneiland, Eastern Docklands
*Island adventure*

It may take some effort (reservations
are recommended a month in
advance) but Vuurtoreneiland is
worth it. The experience starts with
a ferry ride to Lighthouse Island,
a Unesco World Heritage site, on
IJmeer Lake. In winter guests dine
in a 19th-century fort; in summer
the feast moves to a greenhouse
to maximise the view. The
European set menu focuses on
food prepared using traditional
techniques: think sheep's cheese,
buck meat and wild garlic.
*Boats depart from opposite Lloyd
Hotel, 34 Oostelijke Handelskade,
1019 BN
+31 (0)20 362 1664
vuurtoreneiland.nl*

**①**
Lot Sixty One, Oud-West
*Much-loved micro-roastery*

Because they roast on-site, the air
at Lot Sixty One is always heavy
with the scent of coffee: rich and
earthy with a hint of chocolate.
The menu focuses on beans from
small farms such as Finca Toño
in Costa Rica's West Valley and
changes seasonally according
to the harvest.
   This is a great place to grab
a velvety-black espresso when
en route to the nearby shops
at De Hallen. But it's also equally
suited to hunkering down with
a cappuccino, a pastry and a
book for an hour or two.
*112 Kinkerstraat, 1053 ED
+31 (0)61 605 4227
lotsixtyonecoffee.com*

**②**

Scandinavian Embassy, De Pijp
*World view*

The Argentinean-Swedish-Polish team behind this shop are serious about coffee. Their weekly changing menu specialises in filter coffee and they buy everything from a network of roasteries across Scandinavia, which source beans from all over the world.

But this place isn't just about espresso. The owners are on a mission to explore the coffee plant's full potential, serving coffee-flower tea and even coffee-pickled oysters. They also have a few Scandi treats, including meatballs, *øllebrød* (beer-and-bread porridge) and rye bread.
*34 Sarphatipark, 1072 PB*
*+31 (0)61 951 8199*
*scandinavianembassy.nl*

**③**
Grand Café Beurs van Berlage, Centrum
*Historic setting*

The Beurs van Berlage building (*see page 112*), which was designed by prominent Dutch architect HP Berlage in 1903, was seen as the beginning of modern architecture in the Netherlands. The room that now holds the Grand Café Beurs van Berlage was originally the stately entrance and the art nouveau interior includes wonderful brickwork and tile tableaux by Dutch-Indonesian artist Jan Toorop depicting his interpretation of the past, present and future.

Inexplicably overlooked by the tourist hordes, this is a quiet spot for a well-poured Illy coffee and some simple Dutch food. In the summer the tables spill out onto a large terrace on the sun-drenched Beursplein.
*1-3 Beursplein, 1012 JW*
*+31 (0)20 530 4146*
*beursvanberlage.com*

**Must-try**
Apple pie at Café Papeneiland
This dessert has been a favourite with the Dutch since the Middle Ages. This version is homemade, unfussy and famous (Bill Clinton stopped by for a taste), with a golden-brown crust and layers of moist apples.
*papeneiland.nl*

④
Toki, Jordaan
*Easy does it*

This light-filled hangout offers a superb range of coffee from Berlin roastery Bonanza, with an ever-changing selection of beans. Order a flat white and a slice of fresh lemon-drizzle cake and sink into the large sofa along with the rest of the neighbourhood. This is a place to take it easy.

Owner Jeff Flink (*pictured, on left*) has also created a brew bar for his Bellocq tea menu, key for the perfect cup of Lapsang Souchong or Alpine herbal blend *pic du midi*. For something harder there's a fridge full of half-litre beers.
*15 Binnen Dommerstraat, 1013 HK*
*+31 (0)20 363 6009*
*tokiho.amsterdam*

Everyone's happy
—
Toki also caters for tea and beer drinkers

### Baked goods

**01** **Hartog's Volkoren Bakkerij en Maalderij, Oost:** The Hartog family's wholemeal loaves have been drawing queues of people for more than a century. Try the sunflower-seed bread for extra crunch or the *gevulde koeken* (almond cookies) for a traditional Dutch snack.
*volkorenbrood.nl*

**02** **Bakken met Passie, De Pijp:** After visiting Albert Cuypmarkt (*see page 41*), drop into this café for a rest and a bite to eat. Its croissants, cooked the French way, are buttery, flaky perfection.
*bakkenmetpassie.nl*

**03** **De Laatste Kruimel, Centrum:** Every last crumb tends to disappear at this much-loved bolthole in the centre of town. It's more of a takeaway place so grab a slice of freshly baked quiche or order a piping hot toastie and eat it by the canal.
*delaatstekruimel.nl*

## Food markets and retailers
Gourmets galore

### ① Fromagerie Abraham Kef, Jordaan
*Speciality cheese*

You can't cross a canal without running into a cheese shop in Amsterdam but Kef is one of a kind. There's plenty of top-notch French fromage but go for the Dutch *kaas* (cheese). Even though the selection is small it's from the country's best producers, and the staff will happily talk you through the range.

Since 2000, owner Marike van der Werff (*pictured*) has been handpicking whatever she likes each season and selling it alongside delicious fig bread, pâté and pickles. Book a month in advance for the Sunday tasting sessions.
*192B Marnixstraat, 1016 TJ*
*+31 (0)20 420 0097*
*abrahamkef.nl*

**②** De Pasteibakkerij, Rijnbuurt
*Meat-lovers' paradise*

Floris Brester and Diny Schouten (*both pictured*) are determined to revive the Netherlands' charcuterie tradition, using parts of animals – mainly Dutch pigs – that are often overlooked. As well as terrines, rillettes and pâtés made with anything from pigs' trotters to "pest" geese culled at Schiphol Airport, they also sell white pudding, sausages and smoked calf's tongue, among other things.

The pair smoke everything themselves in their tiny shop, which is tucked away on a quiet street and only open on Fridays and Saturdays. A hidden gem.
*2 Hoendiepstraat, 1079 LT*
*+31 (0)65 347 5512*

**Must-try**
**Bitterballen at Café de Pels**
*Bitterballen* are the centrepiece of any Dutch evening gathering (known as a *borrel*) and with good reason. Hidden inside the crunchy, golden exterior of these deep-fried balls is a rich, gooey roux flecked with meat. Dip them in some sharp mustard for the full effect. Veal *bitterballen* from Holtkamp are among the best and the elegant Café de Pels, which dates back to the 1960s, is a great place to enjoy them.

Other traditional *borrelhapjes* (*borrel* snacks) to enjoy with a drink include *garnelenkroketten* (prawn croquettes) and *ossenworst* (raw beef sausage). Or try the *borrelbord*, featuring top-notch terrine from De Pasteibakkerij (*see page 40*). *cafedepels.nl*

(3)
Noordermarkt, Jordaan
*Farmers' market*

Every Saturday the Noordermarkt's large food section opens to the public. Bustling with people who come from far and wide, this is a great place to grab some fresh, seasonal produce.

It's a one-stop shop for the ultimate picnic or dinner party: truffle ravioli, raw-milk butter, juicy dates, colourful displays of vegetables, fresh oysters, Dutch cheese, fragrant herbs – and everything is organic. There's also an adjoining flea market on Mondays where you can pick up antique sunglasses, rare books, old records and other curiosities.
*Noordermarkt, 1015 MV*
*noordermarkt-amsterdam.nl*

Foodhallen, Oud-West
*The spice of life*

Foodhallen food market is the star attraction in the cleverly renovated De Hallen complex. It isn't huge but the market is bordered by stalls serving everything from prawn-tempura buns to raw salad bowls, and there are shared tables dotted through the centre.

Kick a hangover with a sausage, bacon and chip roll from Bulls and Dogs, go healthy with *goi cuon* rice-paper rolls from Viet View or try Le Big Fish's Dutch *kibbeling* (battered fried fish). Come for a weekday lunch to beat the crowds and don't miss the gin-and-tonic bar.
*51 Bellamyplein, 1053 AT*
*+31 (0)62 926 5037*
*foodhallen.nl*

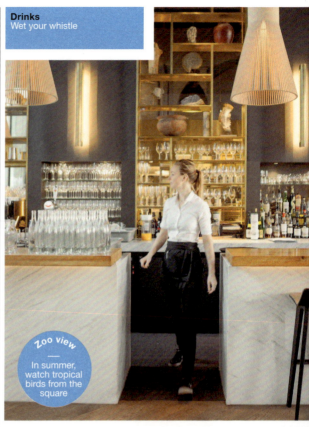

**Zoo view**
——
In summer, watch tropical birds from the square

(5)
Thull's, Oost
*Pickles and preserves*

The first thing you notice is the smell of vinegar. Thull's specialises in all things fermented, pickled and preserved, from jams and gherkins to sardines. It was set up in 2015 by Simone van Thull to share her love of "healthy and colourful" food.

The shop also has a café where you can grab bites such as a smoked trout, pickled fennel and cress sandwich. Make sure you try the most popular product: water kefir. This gut-repairing, gently sparkling punch is produced by mixing water, water kefir grains, dried figs, lemon and sugar.
*69 Pretoriusstraat, 1092 GB*
*+31 (0)20 363 5474*
*thulls.nl*

**1**

Café-Restaurant de Plantage,
De Plantage
*Birdwatching in style*

This soaring conservatory next
to the historic Artis Zoo is a
great spot for a drink. Despite
its spacious interior it feels cosy
in winter, while in the summer
one side opens completely onto a
large tree-lined square where you
can watch the zoo's tropical birds
strutting and preening.

The crowd here is smart,
making it a foolproof option for
drinks with clients in the week. The
extensive wine list is organised by
taste – bright and elegant or earthy
and spicy – and there are eight
different gins. Bar snacks such as
oysters and pork belly are available
when you get peckish.
*36 Plantage Kerklaan, 1018 CZ*
*+31 (0)20 760 6800*
*caferestaurantdeplantage.nl*

**2**

Pont 13, Houthavens
*All aboard*

Built in 1927, this boat spent most
of the 20th century ferrying people
across the IJ but is now anchored
to the remote (by Amsterdam
standards) Haparandadam jetty.
It's worth the journey: the views
are spectacular and the isolated
location makes this place feel
undiscovered.

The industrial interior retains
many of the boat's original features
and the benches on the top deck
are a great place to enjoy a beer.
For food, order the oysters or a
burger. Private events are common
so phone to check opening times.
*50 Haparandadam, 1013 AT*
*+31 (0)20 770 2722*
*pont13.nl*

*If you eat any
more chips you
won't be able
to take off*

### ❸
Wynand Fockink, Centrum
*High spirits*

Before gin there was *genever*. Wynand Fockink serves the juniper-flavoured liqueur, also known as Dutch gin, the old-fashioned way: in a tulip glass filled all the way to the top, so you have to bow to take your first sip.

The lively bar is a *proeflokaal*, or tasting room that dates back to the 17th century, as do the adjoining shop and distillery. The owners produce more than 70 liqueurs, including *Hansje in de Kelder* (Little Hans in the Basement), a celebratory drink tinged with apricot, lemon, orange and cinnamon.

*31 Pijlsteeg, 1012 HH*
*+31 (0)20 639 2695*
*wynand-fockink.nl*

### ④
GlouGlou, De Pijp
*Down-to-earth wine bar*

GlouGlou is out to prove that Amsterdam is not just about beer. The bar serves only natural wine, mainly from Europe, and the staff are happy to advise. With nearly everything available by the glass, you can experiment without breaking the bank.

The pub-style interior and unpretentious approach make this a far cry from conventional wine bars. Throw in snails, cheese boards and fresh bread and you can see why it's a favourite among the De Pijp crowd. There is also a wine shop for takeaways.

*3 Tweede van der Helststraat, 1073 AE*
*+31 (0)20 233 8642*
*glouglou.nl*

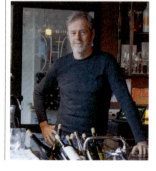

### Complex flavours

If you like your craft beer with oomph, don't miss Oedipus's creative range with delights such as Thai Thai, a tipple with Asian spices. The brewery, off the beaten track in Noord, also serves delicious burgers and makes a great lazy-afternoon destination.
*oedipus.com*

⑤
Café Welling, Oud-Zuid
*Arty party*

*Bruine* cafés – so called due to
their cosy wooden interiors and
nicotine-stained ceilings – are an
intrinsic part of Amsterdam life.
Café Welling is one of the most
charming examples of these shrines
to the Dutch idea of *gezelligheid* (*see
pages 75 to 76*). A favourite among
writers and artists, perhaps because
of its location within earshot of the
wonderful Het Concertgebouw
concert hall (*see page 99*), this small
but atmospheric place is a snug
spot for a few early-evening (or
late-night) beers or some *genever*
with the locals. Portraits of famed
intellectual clientele past and
present line the walls.
    Food at Café Welling is
traditional pub-snack fare – think
basic cheese toasties and boiled
eggs – and live jazz concerts are
often held here.
*32 Jan Willem Brouwersstraat,
1071 LN
+31 (0)20 662 0155
cafewelling.nl*

⑥
Kanarie Club, Oud-West
*Chirpy vibe*

Kanarie Club sits at the end of
the Foodhallen (*see page 41*) inside
the city's former tram depot. By day
it's a relaxed café but at night the
space comes into its own. Join the
trendy Oud-West crowd with an
expertly mixed cocktail and sit in
a cosy cubbyhole on industrial bar
stools by the old tram tracks, or up
in the raised swimming pool area.
No swimming suits are required:
the empty pool is a relic from the
building's past when squatters used
it to gather rainwater. The bright
interior is by design powerhouse
Studio Modijefsky.
*51 Bellamyplein, 1053 AT
+31 (0)20 218 1775
kanarieclub.nl*

### On the tiles

**01  De School, De Baarsjes:**
Housed in an old technical
school, De School's
nightclub has a capacity
of 700 and focuses on
Amsterdam DJs. With
a gym, concert space,
café and restaurant, the
complex is open 24
hours at weekends
(*see page 97*).
*deschoolamsterdam.nl*

**02  Warehouse
Elementenstraat,
Nieuwe-West:** Famous
for raves in the 1990s, this
warehouse has recently
reopened, giving up to
2,500 people the chance to
party to house, techno and
electro in a historic club.
*elementenstraat.nl*

**03  De Marktkantine,
Westerpark:** This venue
dates back to 1936 and
has hosted many live
music and theatre events.
It has been in its current
club-gallery-restaurant
incarnation since 2014 and
has a range of rooms that
provide plenty of scope
for a colourful night out.
It's slated to close in 2019
so make the most of it.
*marktkantine.nl*

**04  Undercurrent, Noord:**
Located in the cutting-
edge NDSM complex,
Undercurrent hosts house
and techno parties and
boasts great views of
the city from its floating
platform in the north of
IJ harbour. It also has an
outdoor terrace extending
onto the water.
*undercurrent.nl*

**05  Shelter, Noord:** Modelling
itself as a Berlin-style
club, this industrial-chic
underground venue north
of the river is a popular
spot for techno, house
and other dance music.
*shelteramsterdam.nl*

# Retail
## —— Fill your tote

Innovative retailers are prospering across Amsterdam's streets and the historical architecture of this fine old city, from heritage banks to canal-front houses, is being reimagined as their playground.

The best businesses here enjoy a global customer mix, which enables entrepreneurs to apply fresh approaches to bricks-and-mortar shopping. It also doesn't hurt that the Dutch are a tasteful bunch. From smart buyers with an eye for the most offbeat fashion to potters crafting quirky ceramics, a quality retail niche has been carved out.

Vintage treasures and new designs are waiting to be discovered here so use these pages as a guide for your jaunt around the city's streets and markets. Fill your tote with everything from books to brogues – and a good bunch of flowers – to brighten your day.

**Concept stores**
Mixed retail

① 
X Bank, Centrum
*Going Dutch*

Inside the design-savvy heritage Kas Bank building in Amsterdam's centre, X Bank provides an engulfing space for those who appreciate great products and thoughtful design. Its abiding mission is to highlight design and fashion brands with distinctly Dutch roots.

From cedar-infused gin made in Amsterdam to Jackie Villevoye's hand-embroidered collection, there are plenty of Dutch goods to fill your suitcase.

*172 Spuistraat, 1012 VT*
*+31 (0)20 811 3320*
*xbank.amsterdam*

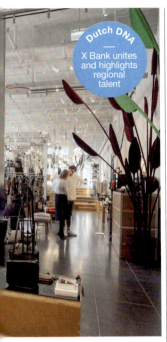

X Bank unites and highlights regional talent

② Hutspot, De Pijp
*Creative gathering*

Named after a traditional Dutch stew, Hutspot is a melting pot of creative talent and promising labels from Amsterdam through to northern Scandinavia. Pick up breezy summer items from Stieglitz or beautiful photos on pinewood by Stiger Woods.

If you're tired of shopping there is a barber on hand and a coffeeshop upstairs; it's staffed by an enthusiastic team who are happy to inform you of book launches and in-store events. There is also a second location in Centrum on Rozengracht.
*4 Van Woustraat, 1073 LL.*
*+31 (0)20 223 1331*
*hutspot.com*

*I'm calling this move the trolley dachshund*

③
### Concrete Matter, Centrum
*In the bag*

"What looks beautiful should be produced in a beautiful way," says Concrete Matter's co-founder Jacob Garvelink. The timber-lined space reflects his good taste and the ambitions of the brand, which caters to men with adventurous spirits.

Everything here is durable and timeless, from Merz B Schwanen shirts to kitchenware from French pocket-knife maker Opinel. Visitors who wish to stock up can take advantage of international shipping for bigger pieces or bulk purchases for their next adventure.

*12 Gasthuismolensteeg, 1016 AN*
*+31 (0)20 261 0933*
*concrete-matter.com*

④
### The Otherist, Centrum
*Curiouser and curiouser*

Inspired by renaissance *wunderkammers* (cabinets of curiosity), The Otherist has been selling trinkets and treasures since 2006. From taxidermy to cardboard creations, the quirky melange of objects reflects the soul of the founders.

"The Otherist is our idea of the world, a microcosm of who we are," says co-founder Joshua Walters. If you're up for a trip down the rabbit hole and have a soft spot for peculiar items, you might never leave.

*6 Leliegracht, 1015 DE*
*+31 (0)20 320 0420*
*otherist.com*

*Robust retail*
—
Get kitted out at Concrete Matter

**Droog, Centrum**
*All under one roof*

This monumental building, which once housed Amsterdam's textile guild, accommodates a variety of sharply designed spaces. Inside you'll find an exhibition gallery, a concept store, a lush garden and a breezy café, all under the auspices of Dutch design company Droog.

The shop stocks everything from iconic Dutch designers such as Marcel Wanders to emerging labels such as Afriek. On the top floor there is also the one-bedroom Hôtel Droog, a bright and airy suite filled, naturally, with Dutch design.

*7B Staalstraat, 1011 JJ*
*+31 (0)20 523 5059*
*droog.com*

**6**
**Restored, Jordaan**
*Take it easy*

Those searching for a keepsake with a clean aesthetic and a good story should look no further than Restored. This pared-down shop stocks plenty of trophies for your home, whether you're into ceramics, quality magazines or textiles from small labels.

Restored stocks minimalist brands such as Royal Republiq for leather goods and Monokel for sunglasses, as well as its own label, which does a smart wireframe plant holder in collaboration with Spitsberg. You'll feel serene and, well, restored after browsing this lovely space.

*39 Haarlemmerdijk, 1013 KA*
*+31 (0)20 337 6473*
*restored.nl*

**1**

ETQ Store, Centrum
*Minimalistic designs*

ETQ's cavernous two-storey space is an ambitious statement from the minimalist men's footwear brand. The label has enjoyed rapid global success since launching in 2010 and no penny has been spared on forming a flagship to match its global prowess.

Designed by Amsterdam's Studio Jos van Dijk, the sprawling polished concrete and raw metal trimmings have transformed a former nightclub into a slick cave for shoes and clothes. The low-cut leather trainers that ETQ is renowned for can be found here but so too can a tight selection of international brands, including Études and Harmony.
*465 Singel, 1012 WP*
*+31 (0)20 261 3815*
*etqstore.com*

**2**

Afura, Oud-West
*Simple pleasures*

Victor ter Hark and Len Koster founded online menswear shop Afura in 2011 and opened this bricks-and-mortar outpost in 2016. The residential neighbourhood may seem an unconventional choice but, flanked by good cafés and inspiring architecture, it's worth the trip.

"We're not a high street shop, our brands don't suit that," says Koster, noting that Afura is the only place in the Netherlands that sells some of the labels stocked here, such as Italian technical outerwear brand Aspesi and offerings from Japan and the US.
*164 Jan Pieter Heijestraat, 1054 ML*
*+31 (0)20 331 3091*
*afurastore.com*

Dress to impress
Head out west for a tight men's edit

③
No Label, Oud-Zuid
*Tailor-made*

No Label aims to take the fuss out of the men's clothes-shopping experience, leaving just well-made, good-fitting fashion. The formula is showcased at the brand's flagship store in the retail district in Amsterdam's south. Here well-appointed staff guide customers to tastefully toned knitwear, classically cut slim suits and a selection of relaxed footwear with prices that are pleasingly friendly on the wallet. For those with a little more time on their hands, No Label also offers a comprehensive tailoring service.
*66 Willemsparkweg, 1071 HK*
*+31 (0)20 846 5591*
*nolabel.nl*

*They say every dog has his day – and this is mine*

Cowboys 2 Catwalk, Centrum
*Prêt à porter*

Cowboys 2 Catwalk rode into town as Amsterdam's exclusive stockist of Comme des Garçons Play in 2006. The shop has grown and today strong Belgian designers, including Dries Van Noten, sit well with Japanese labels.

The shop's buyers have also introduced newer labels to the city, including Russia's subversive Gosha Rubchinskiy. Cowboys 2 Catwalk is smartly divided into three distinct sections with a transparent glass floor, which offers shoppers sweeping views of the brands below.
*107 Utrechtsestraat, 1017 VL*
*+31 (0)20 623 9694*
*cowboys2catwalk.com*

**Mixed fashion**
His and hers

**4**
Salle Privée, Oud-Zuid
*Made to last*

Patrick Munsters rose to prominence as the co-owner of Dutch fast-fashion pioneer Scotch & Soda but his menswear label Salle Privée is a slower-minded beast. His first collection was in collaboration with another Dutch fashion figurehead: Ulrika Lundgren of Rika Studio (*see page 54*).

The high-end brand is all about timelessness; think classic pieces and quality textiles. As the year rolls on the range is updated but all its clothes are designed to endure. The flagship has an equally fastidious approach to lasting excellence.
*9 Cornelis Schuytstraat, 1071 JC*
*+31 (0)85 016 0539*
*salle-privee.com*

**Good jeans**

Olaf Hussein made a name for himself as a cutting-edge denim designer, selling primarily online and gradually expanding his product range. In 2016 he opened a sleek timber-clad boutique, which will appeal to lovers of denim and sharp interiors.
*olafhussein.com*

**1**
The Pelican Studio, Centrum
*The right tone*

Amsterdam fashion retail pioneer Theodoor Kuster was one of the co-founders of this multibrand shop in 2016. Mint green, pastel pink and deep ocean blues provide the backdrop for labels such as Maison Kitsuné, Denmark's Won Hundred, Munich's A Kind of Guise and Sweden's Cmmn Swdn.

"I'm trying to fill the gap between streetwear and high-end," says Kuster, whose other retail venture Velour draws crowds to the busy Huidenstraat. The Pelican Studio is in the Grachtengordel canal ring and worth seeking out.
*35 Raadhuisstraat, 1016 DC*
*+31 (0)20 363 8024*
*thepelicanstudio.com*

②
Teym, Centrum
*No-nonsense necessities*

Housed in a light and airy space
in the heart of Amsterdam, Teym
is a brand that has forged its
identity on structured clothing. The
products are overseen by founder
and designer Maxime Cartens
(*pictured, on left*) and include parkas
designed to endure cold winters,
as well as Italian leather bags.
    Cartens, who has worked with
Karl Lagerfeld and H&M, says she
strives to produce clothes in an
ethical manner. Her slower pace
and careful approach have gained a
dedicated (and patient) following.
*256-1 Nieuwezijds Voorburgwal,
1012 RS
+31 (0)20 261 3876
teym.us*

Margriet Nannings, Centrum
*Laidback browsing*

Designer Margriet Nannings has
built a mini shopping empire on
the Prinsenstraat: one shop for
women, one for men and even
an outlet for bargain hunters.
    The neighbouring shops are
an extension of her personality. "I
care for quality and unique designs
but the colours and styles of other
brands should complement each
other as well," says Nannings. That
down-to-earth nature is apparent
in the labels she stocks, including
APC, Comme des Garçons, Maison
Margiela and her own wares.
*6, 8 & 15 Prinsenstraat, 1015 DC
Women: +31 (0)20 620 7672
Men: +31 (0)20 620 3413
margrietnannings.com*

④
Ennu, Oud-Zuid
*Where fashion meets passion*

High-end fashion for men and
women sits comfortably in this
lavishly designed retailer just off
Van Breestraat, a street for luxury
shopping that you'll find next to
Vondelpark.
    Expect fresh-off-the-runway
looks from the world's best and
most avant garde fashion designers.
Owner and buyer Pieter Baane's
knack for trailblazing comes across
in a retail design that never fails to
surprise, with sprightly art pieces
that adorn its vibrant green walls.
*15 Cornelis Schuytstraat, 1071 JC
+31 (0)20 673 5265
ennu.nl*

Beautiful basics
—
Classic
must-haves,
sustainably
made

## Womenswear
### Wardrobe essentials

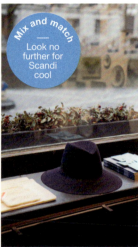

**Mix and match** — Look no further for Scandi cool

② **Rika Studio, Centrum**
*Fashion polymath*

Swedish designer Ulrika Lundgren leads a busy life. A glimpse into it can be had in this charming corner of the Herengracht canal and Oude Spiegelstraat, where Lundgren operates a hotel (*see page 22*), a lifestyle shop and her womenswear label Rika Studio. Her designs tend to balance Scandinavian refinement with bright colours.

Visitors can also grab a copy of *Rika Magazine*, in which editorials showcase the designer's fine work as well as pieces from her favourite brands and photographers.
*9 Oude Spiegelstraat, 1016 BM*
*+31 (0)20 330 1112*
*rikastudios.com*

① **Van Ravenstein, Centrum**
*Grand dame of designer boutiques*

Van Ravenstein is an institution on Amsterdam's fashion scene; the clean interior has hardly changed since this shop opened in 1995. "We pursue timelessness but try to include a surprise factor in our collections and take great care with our choices," says co-founder Linda van Ravenstein. "For instance, I always consider whether pieces can endure a bike ride on the canals."

Van Ravenstein's selection is diverse, with everything from husband and wife design duo AF Vandevorst to labels of the moment such as Vetements.
*359 Keizersgracht, 1061 EJ*
*+31 (0)20 639 0067*
*van-ravenstein.nl*

**In good taste**

Vanilia is arguably one of Amsterdam's most successful womenswear brands. Its on-trend cuts are made in a socially responsible manner and its approach to physical shops is equally noble, repurposing heritage buildings in a sensitive fashion.
*vanilia.com*

**3**
Maha, Centrum
*Street smarts*

This shop takes a novel approach to women's fashion: stock includes feminine streetwear and smaller-sized menswear items. "We started because I was always wearing my boyfriend's clothes as I couldn't buy what I wanted in Amsterdam," says Saskia van Hofwegen, who launched Maha with her boyfriend Dian Iskandar (*both pictured*) in 2015.

With women open to more masculine silhouettes, the shop quickly gained a cult following. Expect to find the latest from Opening Ceremony and Adidas.
*105 Vijzelstraat, 1017 HH*
*+31 (0)20 363 5561*
*shop.maha-amsterdam.com*

Maha's high-quality streetwear is a hit

**Homeware**
Interesting interiors

**1**
Keramiek Atelier Marjoke de Heer, Noord
*Seamless ceramics*

On the outskirts of Noord lies Keramiek Atelier Marjoke de Heer, which was established in 1994. The ceramics collection consists of pieces that are "one of a kind and, above all, made by the same pair of hands," says owner Marjoke de Heer.

Her ceramics are finished with self-developed glazes inspired by ancient Asian traditions. Celadon, Shino, flambé glaze and Temmoku are some of her signature styles. Her beautifully crafted tableware, garden objects and pots range from €10 to €1,000.
*243 Schellingwouderdijk, 1023 NG*
*+31 (0)20 490 4936*
*marjokedeheer.com*

**Shop/Shop, Oud-Zuid**
*Splash of colour*

Shop/Shop is the spot that
Amsterdammers head to when
looking for good design with an
international flair. The neutral
walls and floors make for a perfect
canvas for Dutch product designers
Carole Baijings (*see pages 79 to 80*)
and Stefan Scholten's selection of
colourful tableware.

The shop stocks all of the
pair's work, including partnerships
with potters in the Japanese region
of Arita, from where they have
brought over an inspiring mix
of items.
*2-4 Ruysdaelkade, 1072 AG*
*+31 (0)20 420 8940*
*scholtenbaijings.com*

**③**
**Moooi, Jordaan**
*Throw some shapes*

Moooi specialises in lighting,
furniture and textiles, finishing
most of its pieces with a flamboyant
touch. If you're not afraid of colour
and appreciate humorous design,
make sure you swing by.

The firm, founded in 2001
by Marcel Wanders and Casper
Vissers, exudes avant gardism
and boldness. The duo enjoy
blowing up proportions and
putting their twist on traditional
products. Brands such as Front,
Studio Job and Arihiro Miyake
are sold alongside Moooi's in-
house creations.
*187 Westerstraat, 1015 MA*
*+31 (0)20 528 7760*
*moooi.com*

④
Gastronomie Nostalgie, Centrum
*Treasure chest*

The selection of vintage artefacts in this jam-packed shop is astonishingly diverse – and with price tags to match. Many of the antique items, such as silver candlesticks and porcelain, were originally owned by wealthy Europeans or legendary hotels.

Owner Andre Duijves says he scours international auctions for antique china, glassware and more. "I believe that table decorations are like jewellery for your home," says Duijves, who has an eye for crystal carafes, finely finished whiskey glasses and silver napkin rings.
*361 Nieuwezijds Voorburgwal, 1012 RM
+31 (0)20 422 2167
gastronomienostalgie.nl*

**Bold inspiration**
—
Iconic objects from dozens of designers

Keep it green

Release
your inner
gardener at
Wildernis

 ①

**Tenue de Nîmes, Jordaan**
*Distinctive denim*

Tenue de Nîmes, the go-to jeans
boutique in Amsterdam, is known
for its quality denim selection.
Situated on Haarlemmerstraat since
2012, the shop has a solid range of
labels that is regularly updated.

"Every era can be described
in a signature pair of jeans that
underscores the relevance of this
timeless wardrobe item," says
co-founder Menno van Meurs.
Sitting on raw wooden shelves
in the industrial-style space are
brands such as Acne Studios and
Libertine Libertine, as well as the
shop's own collaborative products.
*92-94 Haarlemmerstraat 92, 1013 EV
+31 (0)20 331 2778
tenuedenimes.com*

**Three more denim emporiums**

**01**  **Mick Keus, Centrum:**
Mick Keus unites the
old with the new by
customising vintage
Levi 501s. Each pair is
unique; just pop in and
find your size.
*mickkeus.nl*

**02**  **Denim City, Oud-West:**
Among the city's many
denim-driven concepts,
Denim City is a whole new
breed. On weekdays it's
an innovation centre,
archive and workplace; at
the weekend it's a shop
with a tailor who adjusts
your denim on the fly.
*denimcity.org*

**03**  **Tossijn, Centrum:** Koen
Tossijn, led by a desire for
durability and quality,
stocks easy-to-wear
Japanese denim.
*tossijn.com*

② 

**Wildernis, Oud-West**
*Urban jungle*

Terracotta pots, tiny cacti and
house plants are artfully arranged
around this lovely shop. A hub
for urbanites wanting a bit of
greenery for their homes, Wildernis
demonstrates what is possible
even in the smallest of spaces.

"There's a growing realisation
that our city is getting busier
and we have to take care of it
and make sure the environment
stays green for everyone," says
co-founder Mila van de Wall.
"People are also realising that
plants in the house are important
for their health."
*165F Bilderdijkstraat, 1053 KP
+31 (0)20 785 2517
wildernisamsterdam.nl*

## Marie-Stella-Maris, Centrum
### *Thirsty work*

Marie-Stella-Maris opened in 2014, inspired by a social incentive to support water projects around the world. The two-storey flagship immaculately displays a selection of room sprays, perfumes and natural skincare products. For each Marie-Stella-Maris item purchased, a fixed amount is donated to a clean drinking-water project.

Greenery, eye-catching typography and well-placed mirrors enliven the shopping experience and a passionate team is on hand to explain the brand's unique mission.
*357HS Keizersgracht, 1016 EJ*
*+31 (0)85 273 2845*
*marie-stella-maris.com*

*Buy the whole bunch and maybe I'll let you buy me a genever too*

### Good for the soles

Famed trainer boutique Solebox is a mecca for sneakerheads but you'll easily mistake this outpost for a laboratory. The clinically clean environment creates the perfect backdrop for a selection of high-tops and low-cut trainers to suit all tastes.
*solebox.com*

Ⓒ
Tommy Page, Centrum
*History boy*

From the best British tweed jackets
to durable knitwear, quality men's
vintage is sold at this well-stocked
establishment, which sits in the De
9 Straatjes shopping precinct.

Owner Tommy Page is typically
on hand to lend sartorial advice.
His opinion is one to be trusted
too, as the fashion designer turned
vintage purveyor is an expert on
the various cuts and styles of all
ages of fashion, from Victorian
rowing jackets to mod suits, all
of which are available here.
*7 Prinsenstraat, 1015 DA*
*+31 (0)20 330 7941*
*tommypage.nl*

---

### Secondhand and vintage

**01 Salon Heleen Hülsmann,
Oud-Zuid:** You won't
be disappointed here. Find
secondhand high-end
designer gems from
recent collections.
*salonheleenhulsmann.nl*

**02 Second New Wardrobe,
Centrum:** Second New
Wardrobe offers barely
worn designer clothing,
as well as samples
straight off the runway.
*324HS Kerkstraat, 1017 HC*

**03 De Ruilhoek, De Pijp:**
De Ruilhoek's charm lies
in its friendly staff and
jam-packed space. You
really need to dig around
but if you don't mind
rolling up your sleeves you
might just end up with a
designer jewel for a steal.
*deruilhoek.nl*

---

④
Pompon, Jordaan
*Bloomin' marvellous*

In a city flowering with florists,
Pompon stands out as one of
Amsterdam's best and most
adventurous. The rich, intense
colours and arrangements often
bring to mind the paintings of
17th-century Dutch masters.

Co-owners Hilde Baart
(*pictured*) and husband Joost are
constantly searching for interesting
forms of floral expression and
specialise in hand-bound bouquets
of wildflowers. "After almost 30
years of running this business I still
get excited about a small, freshly
cut bunch of rare flowers," she says.
*8-10 Prinsengracht, 1015 VD*
*+31 (0)20 622 5137*
*pompon.nl*

⑤
Ace & Tate, Centrum
*Clear vision*

Puns aside, eyewear retailer Ace
& Tate is a visionary brand. Its
idea to cut the excess out of the
industry and deliver fashionable
yet affordable glasses has led to its
rapid success. What started as an
online-only service now has three
outposts across Amsterdam but the
attractive price point and quality
haven't changed.

The brand's sleek Centrum
outlet offers eye tests and one-
hour services for prescription-lens
fittings. The handsome frames are
displayed on shelves designed by
Dutch agency Occult Studios.
*20 Huidenstraat, 1016 ES*
*+31 (0)20 261 8920*
*aceandtate.nl*

**Books and records**
Type and tunes

**②**
Mendo, Centrum
*Creative credentials*

Co-founded by entrepreneur
Roy Rietstap and graphic designer
Joost Albronda, and designed
by Concrete Architectural
Associates, this inky interiored
shop stocks an impressive
collection of beautiful titles.
  Pick up the finest books
on photography and fashion –
such as monographs of Henrik
Purienne, Mario Testino and Carli
Hermès – as well as those on the
art of interior and graphic design,
travel and cooking. Don't miss
Mendo's in-house imprint either.
*11 Berenstraat, 1016 GG
+31 (0)20 612 1216
mendo.nl*

**①**
Architectura & Natura, Centrum
*Building boom*

While pottering amid the canals,
cobbled streets and handsome
terraces of the city centre,
make sure to stop by bookshop
Architectura & Natura. Titles cover
varied subjects such as urbanism
and landscape gardening and are
available in Dutch and English
  The shop also publishes tomes
on architecture, from reference titles
on FA Warners who rose to fame
in the Amsterdam School to books
on urban renewal. There's plenty
here not just for the professional
architect but for those who have an
appreciation of the form.
*22 Leliegracht, 1015 DG
+31 (0)20 623 6186
architectura.nl*

## Record shops

Synonymous with good music, Amsterdam is a magnet for vinyl collectors. The availability of both new and used records is dizzying.

**01 Waxwell Records, Centrum:** As well as selling records from hip-hop to reggae, this shop connects customers with collectors and can take old LPs off your hands.
*waxwell.com*

**02 Second Life Records, Jordaan:** As its name suggests, this is where record fans can resurrect used vinyl and CDs from a cluttered collection of myriad genres.
*secondlifemusic.nl*

**03 Redlight Records, Centrum:** Ring the buzzer and enter a bordello of good music, where funk, jazz, progressive, world, pop, rock, wave, disco and house albums circulate under moody lighting.
*redlightradio.net/residents/red-light-records*

**04 Vintage Voudou, Centrum:** This is where Amsterdam's DJs come in search of tropical sounds that are becoming increasingly in vogue, from the Caribbean to Caracas.
*vintagevoudou.com*

*By the time this record's stopped spinning I'll have bought 45 more*

**③**

### Rush Hour Records, Centrum
*On the record*

Don't be fooled by the look and feel of this record shop. Rush Hour Records might appear to be all about electronic music but it stocks an extremely broad spectrum of genres, from mellow bossa nova to upbeat synth pop.

Founded in 1997, the label and shop have evolved into a sanctuary for music enthusiasts who come here from far and wide. Its selection of collectables and hard-to-find gems underscores why nothing beats browsing in person. The staff's involvement and passion is what sets the shop apart.
*116 Spuistraat, 1012 VA*
*+31 (0)20 427 4505*
*rushhour.nl*

**④**

### Athenaeum Nieuwscentrum, Centrum
*Best of print*

Since this print treasure trove opened in 1969, its stock has reflected its changing clientele. "In the beginning we had a lot of political magazines: there was a Peru bulletin, a Nicaragua bulletin and squatter literature – strange magazines," says Guus Thijssen, the manager and longest-serving staffer.

Today a strong graphic-design scene in the Netherlands has upped the number of independent magazines here but everything from Belgian art titles to US weeklies are available on the heaving shelves.
*14-16 Spui, 1012 XA*
*+ 31 (0)20 514 1470*
*athenaeum.nl*

**⑤**

## The American Book Center, Centrum
*Bibliophiles delight*

Home to one of the largest collections of English literature in continental Europe, The American Book Center started off as a small bargain bookshop in 1972.

Today literary classics and poetry sit side by side with manga, science fiction and new-age titles. Each section is curated by its own buyer, who is "a matchmaker between ideas and the readers", according to co-owner Lynn Kaplanian. The shop also features an Espresso Book Machine that allows on-demand book printing.
*12 Spui, 1012 XA*
*+31 (0)20 625 5537*
*abc.nl*

### Vintage markets

**01 Noordermarkt, Jordaan:** On Mondays you'll find antiques, textiles and records. On Saturdays Noordermarkt sells organic fruit, vegetables and candles (*see page 41*).
*noordermarkt-amsterdam.nl*

**02 IJ-Hallen, Noord:** The biggest flea market in Europe takes place15 times a year and offers 25 tennis courts' worth of secondhand goods.
*ijhallen.nl*

**03 Waterloopleinmarkt, Centrum:** Shoppers come here for jewellery, bags, bikes and other bits and bobs. Someone once picked up a painting by artist Karel Appel for just a couple of euros, so who knows what you might find.
*waterlooplein.amsterdam*

Meet the writers
——
Come for readings and book signings

# Things we'd buy
—— Talking shops

Dutch design tends to teeter on the line between intrinsically practical and brazenly playful. Neon printed blankets and tea towels spun from the plushest of fabrics, teardrop-shaped hot-water bottles in fuzzy felt, a book the size of your palm and dainty ceramic coffee cups inspired by pleated paper: there are plenty of good-looking, intelligent products to take home.

Of course, you can't leave the Dutch capital without picking up one or two of the classics as well, from handsome bike accessories to fresh tulips, cumin-spiced cheese, *genever* and Dick Bruna's *Miffy* (or *Nijntje*, as she's known to the Dutch) books. Start shopping and fill your luggage with some of our top picks.

01 Bicycle bell and saddle by Veloretti *veloretti.com*
02 K Tiktak's Thee en Koffiehandel Namiddag Thee *tiktak-koffie.nl*
03 Tony's Chocolonely chocolate from Tony's Store *tonyschocolonely.com*
04 De Ruijter chocolate sprinkles from Albert Heijn *ah.nl*
05 KLM Delft Blue houses from Giftshop Souvenirs Kaaks *giftshopkaaks.nl*
06 Tulips from Pompon *pompon.nl*
07 Chocolate by Urban Cacao *urbancacao.com*
08 Rademaker Haagsche Hopjes from Albert Heijn *ah.nl*
09 BeepEgg Amsterdam egg timer from X Bank *xbank.amsterdam*
10 Peanut butter by De Pindakaaswinkel *depindakaaswinkel.nl*
11 Potverdorie pickles and Dutch cheese from Fromagerie Abraham Kef *abrahamkef.nl*
12 Stroopwafel by Original Stroopwafel *+31 (0)61 234 5678*
13 Liqueur and genever by Wynand Fockink *wynand-fockink.nl*
14 Stad & Vat whiskey from Hutspot *hutspot.com*
15 Beer by Brouwerij 't IJ *brouwerijhetij.nl*
16 *Nijntje (Miffy)* by Dick Bruna from Athenaeum Boekhandel *athenaeum.nl*
17 Menswear by Salle Privée *salle-privee.com*
18 Paper Porcelain coffee cups by Scholten & Baijings from Shop/Shop *scholtenbaijings.com*
19 Hot-water bottle by Droog *droog.com*
20 Trainers by ETQ *etqstore.com*

21 Bone porcelain cups
from Hutspot *hutspot.com*
22 Mae Engelgeer tea towels
from Restored *restored.nl*
23 Leather briefcase by
Travelteq *travelteq.com*
24 Glasses by Ace & Tate
*aceandtate.nl*
25 The Cool Club playing
cards from Hutspot
*hutspot.com*

26 Irma Boom-designed museum
guide from Rijksmuseum
*rijksmuseum.nl*
27 *Irma Boom: The Architecture
of the Book* from Athenaeum
Boekhandel
*athenaeum.nl*
28 Vintage scarf from Tommy
Page *tommypage.nl*
29 Vintage film poster from
Eye Filmmuseum *eyefilm.nl*

30 Taiko's Gin by
Conservatorium Hotel
*conservatoriumhotel.com*
31 *Bedankt Sorry Hoeral* Dutch
phrase book from Sissy-Boy
*sissy-boy.com*
32 Jeans from Tenue de Nîmes
*tenuedenimes.com*
33 Scholten & Baijings Colour
Plaid blanket from Shop/Shop
*scholtenbaijings.com*

# 12 essays
—— All about Amsterdam

**①**

Mind your head
*Walking with giants*
*by Pauline den Hartog Jager,*
*journalist*

**②**

Movie nights
*Sophisticated cinema*
*by Brian Maston,*
*film festival co-director*

**③**

Wheels of fortune
*Cycling in the city*
*by Joleen Goffin,*
*Monocle*

**④**

Dutch masters
*We need your help*
*by Hans den Hartog Jager,*
*art critic*

**⑤**

Finding 'gezellig'
*A feel for the city*
*by Venetia Rainey,*
*Monocle*

**⑥**

Life goals
*Lesson in football*
*by Dan Poole,*
*Monocle*

**⑦**

'Dam creative
*The city's design scene*
*by Carole Baijings,*
*designer*

**⑧**

Land, liberals and Lennon
*History in a nutshell*
*by Mikaela Aitken,*
*Monocle*

**⑨**

From silk to silicon
*Next-generation start-ups*
*by Yoko Choy,*
*journalist*

**⑩**

What's your type?
*Every letter tells a story*
*by Ramiro Espinoza,*
*type designer*

**⑪**

After dark
*The night manager*
*by Mirik Milan,*
*night mayor*

**⑫**

Full circle
*Dutch food gets a makeover*
*by Vicky Hampton,*
*food writer*

*What better way*
*to discover the*
*city than by*
*hammock?*

# Mind your head
## *Walking with giants*

On the streets of Amsterdam you won't struggle to identify the towering locals from the tourists. The country may be small in surface area but the residents are shooting up to rank as one of the tallest populations worldwide.

*by Pauline den Hartog Jager, journalist*

More than half of the Netherlands lies below sea level and, besides building better dykes to protect the country from the encroaching water, we Dutch have found a natural way to survive global warming: by making sure our heads are above water.

It's no secret that the Dutch are a lanky lot. With an average height of 1.83 metres, Dutch men are the world's tallest, while Dutch women (1.7 metres) are second only to their Latvian counterparts. If you're still not convinced, the Club for Tall People in the Netherlands requires its female members to be taller than 1.8 metres and male members taller than 1.9 metres. There are about 900,000 people in the Netherlands taller than 1.9 metres and an astounding 60,000 of them are more than 2 metres tall.

Visitors to the Dutch capital can experience subtle knock-on effects from walking among giants. Bathroom mirrors and showerheads are almost unreachable and attending a concert can offer little more of a view than the shoulders in front of you. But don't worry, you're not alone.

I'm 1.78 metres tall and am by far the shortest in my family. My younger sisters are 1.83 metres and 1.87 metres, with my parents somewhere in between. To greet my cousins with the customary three kisses, I have to strain to reach their towering frames (1.97 metres and 2.05 metres respectively). It wasn't until I moved to the UK that I realised I'm not that short at all by non-Dutch standards. I often get asked to grab something from the top shelf in the supermarket and standing in a packed Tube is far less claustrophobic when you are able to catch some air.

Still, I have no reason to complain about my height: I fit most regular-sized clothes, my shoe size is about average, I can ride a bike with a regular frame and I won't hit my head when entering a house. Many Dutch citizens, however, face height-related challenges on a daily basis. Where to buy shirts that aren't crop tops? How to find a zippy city car with enough legroom? The real issues start when we travel abroad: urinals are too low, showerheads neglect anything above chest height and beds are too short. It can also be a painful experience: I once ended up with concussion after smashing my head against a ceiling beam.

**High and mighty**
—
01 **Tijs Verwest, 1.88 metres**
Famous DJ, known as DJ Tiësto.
02 **Famke Janssen, 1.82 metres**
Actress and former Bond girl in *Goldeneye*.
03 **Rob Bruintjes, 2.21 metres**
Chairman of the Dutch Foundation for Tall People.

*"Bathroom mirrors are almost unreachable and attending a concert can offer little more of a view than the shoulders in front of you"*

Luckily for its giants, the Netherlands has solutions: bikes come in different frame sizes, more fashion brands produce longer jeans and higher kitchen tabletops are becoming the homeware shop default. There are also support groups, organisations, and magazines dedicated to the extremely tall. Among them, Stichting Lange Mensen (Foundation for Tall People) and Klub Lange Mensen (Club for Tall People) help support the rights of the Dutch giants, including their ongoing battle for more legroom on airplanes.

The Netherlands also ranks as one of the nations that produces the most top models but you won't spot many locals wearing killer heels; trainers are perfectly acceptable in most bars and pubs. Even the policymakers are helping out: in 2003 the minimum ceiling height for new-build houses was increased from 2.4 to 2.6 metres.

The Dutch haven't always been so lofty. The average male height today is 20cm higher than 150 years ago. But the cause of our long limbs is contentious. Is it genetics, fresh air or healthcare? Are we really evolving in reaction to those rising tides or is it simply our affinity with cheese and milk?

According to recent studies the answer is more obvious: genetics. Tall people tend to marry other tall people and tall men tend to have more children than their shorter countrymen. The curve hasn't slowed, which means plenty more opportunities for inventive solutions to cater to an ever-growing population. In height, that is. — (M)

ABOUT THE WRITER: Pauline den Hartog Jager is a London-based film-maker and journalist and was previously MONOCLE's video journalist. Whenever she returns to the Netherlands she picks up a block (or two) of Old Amsterdam cheese.

ESSAY 02
# Movie nights
## *Sophisticated cinema*

———

Going to the pictures in Amsterdam doesn't have to mean spending time in a modern multiplex. For added nostalgia, follow the locals to an art deco gem – you might even catch a homegrown film.

*by Brian Maston,*
*film festival co-director*

On a sunny day in Los Angeles in 1994, a ponytailed John Travolta describes to Samuel L Jackson the particular joys of going to the cinema in the Dutch capital. "You can walk into a movie theatre in Amsterdam and buy a beer. And I don't mean just, like, no paper cup – I'm talking about a *glass* of beer."

This scene introduces hitmen Jules and Vincent in Quentin Tarantino's neo-noir classic *Pulp Fiction*. Tarantino wrote the script for the film while holed up in the Dutch capital. He immediately recognised the cinema culture in the city as something quite unique when compared with the suburban multiplexes of the time.

In that regard, little about the movie-going experience has changed in Amsterdam since the 1990s – or the 1920s for that matter. While the city has several modern cinemas, its chic, well-heeled youth still tends to prefer the traditional movie houses built in the early 20th century to today's soulless big-box cinemas. Gothic and elegant Tuschinski receives the most attention and is often the site of major Dutch film premieres but cosy neighbourhood cinema The Movies offers an authentic and lively cinematic experience. Housed in a narrow and unassuming shopfront, the venue opens up to reveal four screens and a spacious art deco café and restaurant, along with a candlelit wooden bar. Going to the cinema is a social occasion in Amsterdam and, while informal, no one shows up in a tracksuit. And yes, you can take your beer into the theatre.

Amsterdam's cinemas show a variety of independent and international films, which can make it hard for native-born film-makers to compete. The Dutch film industry has yet to produce a unique international style such as Italian neorealismo or French nouvelle vague. Popular Dutch films tend to mostly reproduce Hollywood genres such as romcoms and action films. At the other end of the spectrum are the festival films that don't reach much of an audience at all beyond critics and film buffs.

But it's no real blow to national pride to point this out: the Dutch are well aware of their film industry's shortcomings. For many years, Dutch films were synonymous with poor acting and gratuitous sex scenes. Since the 1970s, sex has been Dutch film-makers' go-to method for attracting audiences and

> *"Going to the cinema is a social occasion in Amsterdam and, while informal, no one shows up in a tracksuit"*

creating a buzz around their work. One of the more proficient purveyors of this aesthetic is that looming giant of the Dutch film industry, Paul Verhoeven. Sex and sexuality have been recurring themes in his films, from the lauded 1977 Second World War classic *Soldier of Orange* to Golden Globe-winning *Elle*, which was released in 2016.

Verhoeven is one of the few Dutch directors to have "made it big" in Hollywood but, over the years, he's had his share of critics on both sides of the Atlantic. He was more or less exiled to Hollywood in the early 1980s after making some controversial films and in some circles is still remembered for making the worst film of the 1990s: *Showgirls*. But after having built up a career in LA directing blockbusters such as *RoboCop*, *Total Recall* and *Basic Instinct*, he was welcomed home again with open arms.

To a Dutch audience, Verhoeven will most likely be remembered for *Turkish Delight*, a generation-defining film made in 1973 that has contributed to the collective visual consciousness of the Netherlands. The film portrays the tumultuous affair of a young artistic couple, Eric and Olga. It documents their love life in a natural fashion that may be too raw for current audiences accustomed to a more photoshopped version of human intimacy.

Eric and Olga love, fight, kick and scream their way through polite bourgeois society, eventually exhausting each other and the viewer but not before providing one of the most inspiring moments of Dutch cinema: the two of them riding together on one bicycle, laughing and weaving their way through Amsterdam traffic after getting married. The relationship, inevitably, does not last but this iconic image of the two young lovers has survived.

While Verhoeven continues to be relevant even in the twilight of his career, a new generation of Dutch film-makers have stepped up and assumed the reins. They are making films that are both cosmopolitan and local. A good example is Jim Taihuttu's gangster flick *Wolf*, which details the life of a Dutch-Moroccan kickboxer amid the grey landscape of urban Dutch society. The film charts the rise and fall of an immigrant antihero who climbs the socioeconomic ladder like Tony Montana in *Scarface* and punches his way through life like Jake LaMotta in *Raging Bull*. Adaptations from Dutch literature also remain popular, such as the introspective *Tonio*, about love and family tragedy in the Amsterdam literary scene.

Dutch films are becoming more sophisticated and polished, with the old clichés about convenient sex scenes and wooden dialogue slowly disappearing. The country now produces film-makers, documentarians and animators who will some day dominate the silver screens of Amsterdam's sleek cinemas. — (M)

**Top cinemas in Amsterdam**
—
**01 The Movies**
Authentic cinema with a lively bar and restaurant scene.
**02 Pathé Tuschinski**
Classic movie palace in the heart of the city.
**03 FilmHallen**
Neighbourhood cinema with tasty street food.

**ABOUT THE WRITER:** Brian Maston is co-director of CampusDoc Film Festival and a senior lecturer in film and media. He's also a proud resident of Amsterdam, a film buff and someone who is willing to give Verhoeven's *RoboCop* a second chance.

ESSAY 03

# Wheels of fortune
## *Cycling in the city*

———

What's the first thing you do when you arrive in Amsterdam? Get yourself a granny bike, adopt the upright position of a member of the royal family and take control of the road.

*by Joleen Goffin, Monocle*

Call me naïve but as a Flemish-speaking Belgian I thought it was safe to assume that the Dutch and I would have plenty in common. Beyond a border, history and language, it's true that we also share a love of bicycles. From a young age we pedal our way to independence: I was six when I made my first solo journey to school. However, the first time I travelled to Amsterdam to visit a friend, it soon became clear that when it comes to cycling, the Dutch do things differently.

As I confidently mounted my bike at Centraal station, I wasn't prepared for what lay ahead. Almost immediately I was manoeuvred to the side by an overtaking cyclist. I was struck not only by the bravado of the Dutch cyclists but also that of my usually demure friend. With a bluster I had never witnessed she cleared herself a path with voice and bell (I know that's the purpose of a bell but in Belgium it's considered impolite to use it). And as we whisked past unsuspecting tourists, I caught glimpses of their flabbergasted faces. Ten minutes later we arrived. No dawdling – this was serious work.

It's taken a few trips but I think I've finally cracked cycling in the city. It's a thrilling experience to be part of a swarm of starlings moving as if choreographed, crossing busy junctions, navigating our way through the city, weaving between cars and pedestrians. It may seem like chaos to the onlooker but to the participants it's highly organised.

Perhaps the key to success is the Dutch granny bike. It may weigh a tonne but its design ensures that your posture is regimental-straight which, in turn, inspires a new level of confidence: you feel like a royal on a horse. And if you're the queen you don't need a helmet: everyone else will look out for you. It sounds strange but Dutch drivers likely grew up on a bike so they anticipate your behaviour. It's a stark contrast to the slinky Lycra pelotons in cities such as London and New York, always attempting to extract respect from motorists. In Amsterdam it's that posture that makes you feel as if you own the road.

*"It's a thrilling experience to be part of a swarm of starlings moving as if choreographed, navigating our way through the city"*

Or maybe it's the fact that Dutch cyclists don't follow the rules: the rules follow them. I still make mistakes and it's terrifying. On one occasion, while reporting for this guide, I was the first in a queue of bikes waiting at a red light. When I realised I was about to pedal in the wrong direction, I froze. My explanation was lost in the flurry of commuters and I received a grating concerto of bicycle bells and colourful phrases – some of which I didn't even know existed in our language.

This anarchy didn't happen overnight: cycling in the Netherlands has a history. Troops of cyclists would slow down

ESSAY 04

## Pedal to the metal

**01 881,000**
Number of bicycles
in the city.
**02 15,000**
Number of bikes that end
up in the canals each year.
**03 2,000,000km**
Combined distance
cycled by Amsterdammers
every day.

German occupiers during the Second
World War by riding in the middle of the
road but the critical change happened
in the 1970s when the government made
huge investment in infrastructure. For
almost every Belgian this made the
Netherlands a place of pilgrimage to visit
on a cycling holiday. As a kid I remember
knowing the exact moment we crossed
the border: when the bumpy road beneath
our wheels turned to pristine asphalt.

Some argue that Amsterdam has
become a victim of its own success. Bikes
now outnumber people and, if this two-
wheeled transport is not your thing, you
might consider it, as my colleague coined
it bluntly, "bike pollution".

But schemes for more underground
(and underwater) bike parking are being
developed. And all of this feels like a nice
problem to have if you compare it to
capitals where the car is still king. The
health and environmental benefits of
cycling are many but beyond that, there
are few better ways to explore the city.
So when you visit Amsterdam, do as the
locals do and find yourself a granny bike.
Sit up straight, act confident and don't be
intimidated. You'll soon feel the thrill and
blend into the rush of starlings – just don't
freeze at the lights. — (M)

## Dutch masters
### *We need your help*

The Dutch will never
appreciate their own
artists until a foreigner
does. So what are you
waiting for? Hotfoot it
to the city's museums
and galleries and show
your support.

### *by Hans den Hartog Jager, art critic*

Us Dutch have always had a
complicated relationship with our
artistic past. We are a very small
nation, founded on extremely flat
land that for centuries has been
threatened by water. The country
has also been flooded with
something else: Calvinism. These
factors have all left distinctive
traces and it's surely no accident
that one of the most quoted
expressions to summarise the
Dutch national character is: "Act
normal, that's already strange

enough." And then we, as a people, so proud of our normality, produced artists such as Rembrandt (dark and bankrupt), Johannes Vermeer (shy and bankrupt), Frans Hals (almost bankrupt and couldn't draw a straight line) and, well, Van Gogh. Yes, Van Gogh was Dutch.

So it should come as no surprise that it took a fair amount of rumbling and groaning before the Dutch acknowledged the power of our best artists – Rembrandt, the national Calvinistic treasure, being the only exception. At the beginning of the 19th century, after the Netherlands had been ruled by the French for decades, artists such as Hals and Vermeer were collectively all but forgotten. It took a French art critic, Théophile Thoré-Bürger, to point the Dutch back in the direction of their own artistic heritage. Not only did Thoré-Bürger write about artists such as Hals, Vermeer and Fabritius, he also put his money where his mouth was and bought their paintings, including Fabritius's now-famous "Goldfinch" (1654). This was an effective way of

> *"Please, non-Dutch reader, continue to help us. Give us the recognition we need so we can keep appreciating our own artists"*

**Alternative bests**
——
**01 Rembrandt**
"Syndics of the Drapers' Guild" (better than "The Night Watch")
**02 Johannes Vermeer**
"The Milkmaid" (better than "Girl with a Pearl Earring")
**03 Frans Hals**
"Portrait of a Couple" (better than "The Merry Drinker")

persuading the Dutch of his sincerity: the Netherlands, after all, has always been a nation of trade.

Since then this attitude towards Dutch artists has prevailed: everything is poppycock until foreigners say the opposite. The best illustration of this is the story of Paulus Potter's "The Bull" (1647). In the late-18th century this was a moderately appreciated painting until the French invaded, looted some Dutch artwork and carried them to France. "The Bull" was displayed in a prominent spot in the Louvre and everyone fell for the realistic bravado of the painting. After 20 years in France it became a beloved classic – and, of course, that caught the attention of the Dutch. So when Napoleon was defeated, one of the first things the Dutch did was bring "The Bull" home. It was carried to The Hague as part of a large parade, accompanied by military honours and church bells. Only then was a classic born.

Gaining foreign recognition has become standard procedure for a Dutch artist to attract domestic appreciation. Traditionally, most artists of merit don't wait for this and move abroad instead: Van Gogh went to France; Mondrian to France and then the US. In fact, almost every Dutch artist to have become famous has lived abroad, including Willem de Kooning, Karel Appel, Armando, Constant Nieuwenhuys, Bas Jan Ader, Ger van Elk, Daan van Golden, Michael Raedecker and Mark Manders. And the ones who stay tend only to be taken seriously after their first international shows; think of Marlene Dumas (Moma, Tate), Rineke Dijkstra (SF Moma, Guggenheim) and Aernout Mik (Moma). But after that the reward is great and everyone in the Netherlands applauds your success.

So please, dear non-Dutch reader, continue to help us. Give us the recognition we need so we can keep appreciating our own artists. Go to the Rijksmuseum to see Rembrandt, Vermeer, Hals, Fabritius, Dou and Verspronck. Queue in that bloody long line for Van Gogh, one of our national treasures (the line I mean, not the museum). By doing so you help us compensate for our small-country insecurities – and the artwork in the museum is supposed to be great. Or so we are told. — (M)

ABOUT THE WRITER: Hans den Hartog Jager is a writer and art critic based in Amsterdam. He writes for *NRC Handelsblad*, *Artforum International* and various other magazines. He has published more than 10 books, mainly about contemporary art.

ESSAY 05
# Finding 'gezellig'
*A feel for the city*

———

Whether you're out with friends or travelling alone, find yourself a comfy chair in a *bruin* café, order some snacks and chill out. Dutch-style.

*by Venetia Rainey, Monocle*

If there's a word that sums up the best of Dutch culture it's *gezellig*. The under-appreciated sibling of the Danish concept *hygge*, *gezellig* is one of those tangly words whose meaning unravels through experience rather than a neat dictionary definition.

*Gezellig* is an afternoon of games with the family. It's a natter over coffee with an old friend, or laying side by side with your partner in bed reading a book after a long day. It's the neighbour who always stops to say hi or that unpretentious pub where the staff know you by name. It's a plate of deep-fried snacks to share or a cat curling up on your lap when you're ill. Cosy, I think you'll agree, doesn't cover it.

*Gezellig*, or *gezelligheid* to use the noun, doesn't put on airs and doesn't photograph well. It's less concerned with how things look than how they feel and, as such, it will probably never become as fashionable as its Danish counterpart. The Dutch don't mind though: they're too busy enjoying the good things in life to worry about it.

But for any visitor to the Netherlands, understanding *gezelligheid* is crucial and getting yourself into a *hartstikke gezellige* (really *gezellig*) situation should be top of the bucket list. So how to go about it?

> *"The spirit of 'gezellig' is good company, that reaffirming feeling of being in the presence of others, whether you know them or not"*

A good place to start is with a *borrel*, an informal evening gathering with friends (old or new), preferably at an old-school *bruin* café (brown café) such as Café Welling (*see page 45*). Brown cafés, so-called because of the walls and ceilings stained from decades of pre-ban smoking, are temples to the *gezelligheid* doctrine.

Forget about trendy craft beer and fusion bar snacks. These are places for several *fluitjes* (small glasses) of the local pilsner and some traditional Dutch finger food known as *borrelhapjes*. Bitterballen – a deep-fried, golden ball of gooey roux flecked with meat (*see page 41*) – is the king of the *borrelhapjes* but other great contestants include *ossenworst* (raw beef sausage), cubes of old Dutch cheese with some sharp mustard, or a boiled egg.

Travelling solo? Not to worry. Grab a newspaper (or this book) and stake out a corner table at your *bruin* café of choice, being sure to position your chair so you're facing into the room. It's important that you're not closed off from everyone else, even if you don't plan on chatting.

That's because *gezelligheid* isn't all about food and drink. No, the spirit of *gezellig* is good company, that reaffirming feeling of being in the presence of others, whether you know them or not. The word is actually derived from *gezel*, an old term for a companion or fellow that contains the Germanic root *sal*: a place where people gather. The word's meaning has expanded over the past millennium but at its heart *gezellig* still describes a scenario where people take pleasure from being around each other (or even a pet).

Which brings me to *gezellig's* evil twin: *ongezellig*. This should be avoided. It means coming home to a cold, empty house after work and eating alone, or being made to feel unwelcome among friends. Someone using their phone throughout a meal is supremely *ongezellig*, as is a restaurant with unfriendly staff.

While the Dutch can't control the sort of people you hang out with, they are masters at creating the right sort of environment in their restaurants, cafés and bars. Low lighting, comfortable chairs and a warm atmosphere: these are crucial elements of the Dutch hospitality industry (there's a reason Amsterdam is such a joy to wine and dine your way around). All of the food and drink suggestions in this guidebook ooze *gezelligheid* – except for, perhaps, the herring stall, and even that could be *gezellig* if visited on a sunny day.

The only thing left to explain about *gezellig* is how to pronounce it. It's ge-*zell*-ig, and the first and last "g" should come from the back of the throat. If that's too tricky, never mind: it's not as important as actually experiencing it. And the Dutch will always find it *gezellig* that you tried. — (M)

ABOUT THE WRITER: Venetia Rainey is MONOCLE'S Amsterdam correspondent. A radio and print journalist, she recently moved to the Netherlands after several years in the Middle East. She is half-Dutch and thus constantly in search of *gezelligheid*.

---

**'Gezellige' activities**
—
**01 At Noordermarkt**
People-watching and shopping on Saturdays.
**02 In a 'bruin' café**
Playing Rummikub or cards over a few drinks.
**03 In the countryside**
Cycling (*see page 126*) to the north with a friend on a sunny day.

# Life goals
## *Lesson in football*

———

Ajax's reputation for footballing excellence is well established. But could the Amsterdam club also teach the rest of the country a thing or two about societal values?

*by Dan Poole, Monocle*

Granted, it's not often that the words "football team" and "laudable social model" crop up in the same sentence – but they just have so hold on to your hats. Or rather, for the benefit of a drawn-out metaphor, hold on to your crotch. That way I can be the free-kick taker, this essay can be the ball, you can be part of the wall and the goal can be me convincing you that not everything to do with this sport is rotten and fetid.

My instrument of persuasion is Ajax (pronounced "aye-ax") Amsterdam, the Netherlands' most famous club. Its mythical status – it's named after a Greek hero, no less – was sealed at the beginning of the 1970s when it won three European Cups in a row (which doesn't happen very often). The conductor of this footballing symphony was Dutch player Johan Cruyff, who was so talented that he had a move named after him (the Cruyff turn) and is credited with having changed the way that the game is played worldwide.

And here's the thing: such is the manner in which Ajax is run that there are lessons to be learned for the rest of the country. And we're not talking about perfecting a one-touch pass or how to head a ball without falling over; this is about an ethos and vision that applies as much off the pitch as it does on it.

But first let's take a look at an area in which Ajax excels but that the rest of the country needs no help with whatsoever: the recognition that the children are our future. Ajax's world-renowned youth system was set up from the club's inception in 1900 and has been churning out exceptionally talented players ever since – most Dutch and many from Amsterdam or the surrounding area. For example, when the team won the European Cup for a fourth time in 1995,

*"How did this ideology come about, this commitment to not only think of the children but look after employees from top to bottom?"*

eight members of the starting line-up were graduates of the club's academy.

But the Netherlands also scores well in this department. A 2013 Unicef survey established that Dutch children are the happiest in the world, based on metrics including education, health and environment. The country also wins out when it comes to youth unemployment, with two thirds of under-25s in jobs compared with less than half across all OECD-member countries.

So, well played everyone. But it's at the other end of the spectrum that the rest of the country lags behind. A 2016 survey into Dutch people's attitudes towards their older relatives found that two thirds believe it is the government's remit to look after the elderly; indeed, said government is among the top tax spenders in Europe when it comes to senior care. And while Geert Wilders' early-2017 efforts to oust Mark Rutte as PM were divisive at best, one of his claims that most people supported was that the country's elderly are neglected, with risible conditions in many care homes.

Ajax, however, takes a very different approach to its retirees. Now, admittedly we're not talking about OAPs here but the relative brevity of a career in this sport means that footballer years are a bit like dog years. And for most players who have panted their last breath on the pitch, the best they can expect from their parent club is a nebulous ambassadorial role. But Ajax? It gainfully re-employs its elder statesmen.

In recent years Ronald de Boer, his twin brother Frank, Dennis Bergkamp, Jaap Stam and Marc Overmars have all returned to the club where they first made their names. And they've done so having plied their trade abroad – a classic example of a country's talent learning new skills on foreign shores before returning to the motherland to share newfound knowledge. And it's not just in a coaching capacity that they have been deployed; Overmars for example, once a wing wizard, is now technical director.

Then there's Edwin van der Sar. The former goalkeeper was at Ajax for nine years (which included that European Cup win in 1995) before going on to play for Juventus in Italy, then Fulham and Manchester United in England. But once he'd hung up his boots he did a master's in sports and brand management (at the Johan Cruyff Institute in Barcelona, naturally) and then got snapped up by Ajax as its marketing director in 2012.

"I was fortunate enough to return to this club as I owe all of my career to them," he said in 2014. "Now, I have a chance to give it back to the club where it all started. All the former players that are working here with me wanted to contribute at the club that helped us grow as players." The former shot-stopper could clearly walk the walk as well as talk the talk: he was promoted to CEO in 2016.

And how did this ideology come about, this commitment to not only think of the children but look after employees from top to bottom? That man Cruyff again. In 2010 he angrily proclaimed: "This isn't Ajax anymore." Orthodoxy duly challenged, that fabled youth system was refreshed and Van der Sar and friends, former players schooled in the Ajax way, were brought into the fold to inspire the next generation.

So if a system isn't working and a hierarchy has lost its way, the potential for change can be realised? There might well be a lesson for us all there. — (M)

---

### Other things called Ajax

**01 Swedish singer**
Lisa Ajax has a song called "I Don't Give A". Cheeky.
**02 Racehorse**
Won the Grand Prix de Paris in 1904. Magnifique.
**03 Cleaning products**
Pronounced "Ay-jax".
Confusing.

ABOUT THE WRITER: Dan Poole is chief sub editor at MONOCLE and, when not tackling spelling mistakes or giving misplaced commas the red card, likes to watch his beloved Manchester United playing The Beautiful Game (he insisted on those capital letters).

---

ESSAY 07
## 'Dam creative
### *The city's design scene*

———

Amsterdam's natural beauty and artistic heritage make it appealing to visit. And for designers who live and work here it's a constant source of inspiration and community.

*by Carole Baijings, designer*

---

Art and design are inextricably woven into daily life in Amsterdam; we're surrounded by museums housing the works of the most famous Dutch designers and artists. These venues have been part of the city's identity for a long time but other displays of art and design are everywhere, in the form of sculptures, benches, streetlights and great architecture. All of these different aspects fit together and present us with inspiring silhouettes.

Because the Netherlands is so flat it's almost as if the landscape has an ingrained sense of minimalism and I think that is in our DNA. There is a lot of colour around and maybe you see it more because everything is so flat. You see the play of

**Floristry in the city**
———

**01 Pompon**
Wild blooms at their best.
*pompon.nl*

**02 Menno Kroon**
Snap up some
elaborate bouquets.
*mennokroon.nl*

**03 MC Bloom**
Best for potted plants.
*mcbloom.nl*

light with the rising sun and again as it sets, as well as all of the different shades throughout the day, particularly across the canals and IJ harbour. Some of our most revered artists, including Mondrian, Van Gogh, Rietveld and Rembrandt, pioneered the way that the Dutch bring colour into art. All of this culminates to influence the way we work and design here. From the paintings in our galleries to the urban-planning of our neighbourhoods, design in the city is all about light, colour and the contrast between matte and gloss.

Another positive impact of our landscape is its size. The Netherlands is very small so it's easy, even though we're in a capital city, to connect and work closely with the craftsmen who make our prototypes. If you need something or someone, from a textile weaver to a skilled woodworker, you only have to drive for an hour – or three at most – to find it. This combination of the creativity fostered in the city and the skills that exist across the country has created a dynamic design scene in Amsterdam that is hard to come by in other cities. If you live in the centre of London it's much harder to find someone who has a welding factory who can make you a nice frame, or a carpenter you need for a piece of a furniture.

The art and design in our city helps to improve the quality of life and bring together the community. Summer sees the arrival of Art Zuid, when a 2.5km stretch of road is temporarily adorned with sculptures made by international artists;

Schiphol Airport is really close so staying connected with the global design scene is easy. The city also hosts free concerts on the canals, which fill with people in boats, and a hush descends as the floating crowd listens to the orchestra. Then in winter there is the Light Festival, which decorates Vondelpark and the canals with glittering and glowing sculptures.

A good example of what our design heritage means to the people is the area between the Rijksmuseum and the Stedelijk Museum. This space was occupied by a road that ran under the Rijksmuseum; during the renovations to the museum the architects considered closing the passage but Amsterdammers lobbied to keep it open. Today the tunnel is a thoroughfare for cyclists and the space between the museums is a beautiful square full of sporting activities and new buildings, including a supermarket with a green terraced roof for people to enjoy the sun.

We all know each other on the creative scene. We host a lot of lectures here in the Arita House where my husband and I have our showroom and studio, as well as some nice dinners with people from the creative industry. Amsterdam continues to be fantastically inspiring.

Looking forward, the new generation is more focused on materials rather than form and the ones who are really finding their own way are doing things such as making their own machines to produce their own fabrics. They're also recycling a lot of materials and I think that's great. A good example are the glass bricks used by MVRDV in the Hooftstraat Chanel shop; they are very special.

So the city will continue to influence its creatives and in turn the new generation of creatives will influence the city. As a designer, it's a great place to live. — (M)

ABOUT THE WRITER: Carole Baijings and her husband Stefan Scholten run product-design studio Scholten & Baijings, just across from the Rijksmuseum. Their young son Rem is already showing signs of becoming one of Amsterdam's designers of the future.

## ESSAY 08

# Land, liberals and Lennon
## *History in a nutshell*

---

# Founded on commerce that benefitted from dealing with all who docked, Amsterdam's liberal beginnings are still very much part of the city's fabric.

### *by Mikaela Aitken, Monocle*

Some history books would have you believe that Amsterdam was founded by adventurers in hollowed-out logs but most Amsterdammers favour the fable of two fishermen and their dog. The trio were supposedly out on the North Sea when a storm rolled in, so they sought shelter along a stretch of river. Pulling up to land, the woozy hound tumbled from the boat and threw up, thus christening the land for Amsterdam. The factual accuracy of this may be dubious but old versions of the city's crest picture two men and a dog.

In the 12th century, fishermen and farmers encroached the peat swamps surrounding the Amstel river and forged dams and dykes to create low-lying land. One particularly hefty dam across the Amstel is rumoured to have given rise to the name Amsterdam. You can still visit it today although it looks a little different: its modern formation is Dam Square and the main drag, Damrak, sits where the river once ran. From here a medieval merchant town expanded and was granted its first charter in 1300.

Trade of predominantly boats, beer and soused herring fuelled the economy but what really put the city on the map was, once again, vomit. In 1345 a dying man received his final Holy Communion, only to regurgitate the wafer whole. This holy mess was thrown on the fire but the wafer refused to burn. Heralded in likeness to its metaphorical representation of the body of Christ, Catholics declared it a miracle, a church was built on the site and European pilgrims flocked in.

Catholicism grew but the city's leaders practised tolerance, in part owing to open trade and the benefits of business dealings with anyone who docked, regardless of race or religion. Over the coming decades, Spain and the Catholic church tightened their hold on the Netherlands. At this time a young German-born nobleman, Willem of Nassau (or the Prince of Orange), was rising through the ranks of the Spanish court. After seeing the atrocities dealt to Protestants and non-Catholic believers at Spanish hands, he led a revolt and thus began the 80 Years' War, which lasted from 1566 to 1648. In 1584, Willem was murdered in Delft by a devout Catholic but his fight for liberalism inspired a nation and he was memorialised as the father of the Dutch Republic.

Despite the conflict, trade in Amsterdam proliferated. In 1599 the second Dutch expedition to Indonesia returned with a handsome bounty and this new era of commerce sparked the city's Golden Age. Wealth flowed in and the population grew. A new network of canals was added in a ring around the city centre and rows of houses were erected in the 17th century. In one such canal house, Dirck van Os welcomed anyone – Dutch or foreign – wishing to be a shareholder in the Dutch East India Company; this moment was arguably the inception of capitalism. The world's first stock exchange opened in 1602 and in 1655 city hall (now the Royal Palace) was built to tower above the surrounding churches: a sly reminder to the city's clergymen of their inferior role.

Reliance on trade dampened with the industrial revolution in the 19th century, altering the topography of the city. The western entrance to the IJ river was added along with neighbourhoods, including Westerpark and the Eastern Docklands. Leading characters of this era were the coquettish madams of the red-light district. Continuing their historical tolerance, lawmakers turned a blind eye to prostitution (it was only legalised in 2000).

Twentieth-century protagonists continued to guide the narrative of the city, including the architects of the Amsterdam School movement between 1910 and 1930 and banker Walraven van Hall, who led a resistance against Nazi occupation. It was also no accident that John Lennon and Yoko Ono chose Amsterdam as the stage for one of their 1969 bed-ins for peace. They were drawn to the progressive capital, its vibrant population and counterculture movement. Fast-forward to the modern day and these qualities still feel very much part of the city's fabric. Vomit, fable, odd characters and all, Amsterdam continues to uphold its liberal disposition. — (M)

### City of firsts

**01 Modern family**
The 17th-century canal house was arguably the first take on a modern family home.
**02 Pump it up**
The first pump-driven fire hose appeared in 1672.
**03 Love it**
First capital to legalise gay marriage (2001).

ABOUT THE WRITER: As editor of this guide, Mikaela Aitken was raring to explore but she was kind of a wimp when it came to cycling. Instead, she stuck to navigating the canals, cathedrals and queasy tourists on foot – a sensible move, she insists.

ESSAY 09
## From silk to silicon
*Next-generation start-ups*

The brightest technology entrepreneurs are popping up where you would least expect them; Amsterdam is suddenly giving Silicon Valley a run for its money.
*by Yoko Choy, journalist*

Think start-ups and, after Silicon Valley pops into your head, aggressively emerging economies (such as India or China) and traditional major players on the world stage (such as the UK and France) probably come to mind. But a small, northern European city is making a bid to put itself on the map as a major start-up hub – and with impressive results so far.

Better known for their sizeable system of canals, absurd people-to-bike ratio and attitude to work-life balance, it's not as though the Dutch don't have a history of excelling in business. This new entrepreneurial era is a reflection of the early 17th century, when the pioneering nation established the first stock exchange in 1602 and the famed Dutch East India Company dominated trade across the globe.

Four centuries later, the economy is profiting from silicon rather than silk and spices. The Netherlands' latest regeneration began in the late 1990s, with the establishment of start-ups Booking.com and TomTom, two unicorns (technology start-ups valued at more than $1bn) that arose from the capital. At the start of the new millennium the arrival of Adyen, Gemalto and Catawiki reinforced the nation's credentials as a home for fledgling businesses. The Netherlands can offer exemplary travel and logistics infrastructure, proximity to European markets, attractive business tax regulations and, on top of that, the fact that English is widely spoken. All this, plus a general reputation for openness and liveability, have made Amsterdam a magnet for global companies: Netflix, Uber and Tesla have all chosen the canal city for their European headquarters.

The politician who played a leading role in making the Netherlands Europe's start-up hub is Neelie Kroes, the former European commissioner for the digital agenda. Appointed as the special envoy for start-ups in 2014, she led the launch of StartupDelta, an initiative to connect government, start-ups, corporates, universities, research centres and investors. Amsterdam now lays claim to being the continent's best-connected and largest ecosystem for new technology businesses.

*"Making money often doesn't seem to be the new entrepreneur's number-one priority; ideas – and harnessing them to make a better world – are of greater interest"*

Kroes's successor, Prince Constantijn of the Netherlands, has come to his new job with even more ambitious plans. His challenge is to push start-ups to scale-ups. "People need to believe that they can grow really big," he says. "What we are looking at is not the café at the corner but the new Starbucks. We have a few companies that we call unicorns but they are very focused

**Gear about town**
——
**01 Pedal power**
A bike: to take you to meetings across town in 15 minutes.
**02 Look the part**
Ace & Tate glasses: for hours working in front of a screen.
**03 Let off steam**
Membership at private members' club A'Dam&Co: for work-life balance.

on delivering. Once they launch an IPO [an Initial Public Offering: the first sale of stock by a company to the public], those people and the money they made will come back to the ecosystem. You will start to see more of the entrepreneurs who are starting to drive the system."

The new way of doing business – casual, collaborative and light years from traditional hierarchical structures – can be seen in B Amsterdam, a 40,000 sq m co-working space in the central business district that is home to about 250 companies. "The idea is to create a buzz and a physical space where you can bring people together, to create a network of sharing, mentoring and evolving," says co-founder Guus Meulendijks. Last year, in collaboration with the City of Amsterdam, it launched BSSA (B Startup School Amsterdam). The idea is to tackle youth unemployment and a lack of talent in the start-up arena by providing free education and commercial matchmaking.

Further evidence of Amsterdam's grand plans is the launch of Scale (Startup City Alliance Europe). Major hubs such as London, Berlin, Paris, Barcelona, Helsinki, Stockholm, Rome, Brussels, Oslo and Lisbon have already signed up. The idea is to unite municipal governments, corporations and institutions to help companies link up with their neighbouring markets.

The country's small population pushes start-ups to think globally from the outset. One of its best-known successes is large file-sharing tool WeTransfer; following its conception in 2009 it is now used in 190 countries. Co-founder Nalden says: "Berlin is affordable, London has the capital and is often used as a hub of US-based venture capitals or enterprises, and we sit nicely in between the two. Now that the future of the EU is shifting this might be very positive for Amsterdam as we will definitely see some of that money moving here."

Despite the often-unthinkable sums to be made from ingenious start-ups, making money often doesn't seem to be the new entrepreneur's number-one priority; ideas – and harnessing them to make a better world – are of greater interest. An ethical example is the mobile-only challenger bank Bunq. In 2013, Ali Niknam founded the first greenfield bank (a start-up with no history in the field) to operate under a full Dutch banking licence in more than 35 years. "Our ideology is to make banking serve people again; we don't invest with your money and we don't trade your personal data," he says. The integrated banking app has been rolled out in Germany and Austria.

There are many more names to look out for in the future: Vandebron is a green-energy company connecting users directly with suppliers; StuDocu enables people to access and share study resources; and 3D Hubs provides an online 3D-printing service platform. Start-ups, it seems, will cease to emerge only when imagination and ambition run out. — (M)

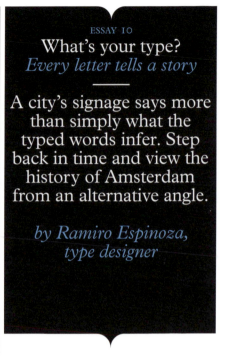

ESSAY 10
## What's your type?
*Every letter tells a story*

A city's signage says more than simply what the typed words infer. Step back in time and view the history of Amsterdam from an alternative angle.

*by Ramiro Espinoza, type designer*

I'm a type designer: someone who earns a living designing fonts. It's an offbeat profession. Type designers can behave like eccentric astronomers or entomologists, focusing on the specimens no one else would even notice or rhapsodising about an unexpected find. But professional oddities aside, the fact is this: as a type designer I know how to interpret meanings and narratives encoded in letterforms.

So I'd like to invite you on a different kind of tour of Amsterdam: an exploration of the city's monumental lettering and hand-painted signs. Doesn't that sound slightly more tantalising than the usual tourist trail?

**ABOUT THE WRITER:** Yoko Choy is a journalist and marketing consultant living between Amsterdam and Hong Kong. She enjoys the city's creativeness but sometimes finds it hard to balance Dutch plain-speaking with the Chinese imperative to "give face".

I promise you that fascinating stories lurk behind Amsterdam's humble letters.

Let's start with those famous bridges. Most of the iron bridges in the city centre feature cast nameplates (Oranjebrug, for example). The letters on these nameplates were designed by the municipality's Public Works department in about 1930. Their quirky design – a compelling mix of organic and geometric elements – originated in the aesthetic ideals championed by the Amsterdam School (*see pages 112 to 113*), a progressive and socially conscious group of architects who, between 1910 and 1930, designed iconic buildings and working-class housing estates.

Now these *Amsterdamse brugletters* (bridge letters) are celebrated as one of the strongest elements of Amsterdam's visual identity. The bridge-style lettering crops up in the logos of many businesses across the city and variations of this font now also appear on several concrete bridges throughout Amsterdam. The Blauwbrug over the Amstel River and the Vondelbrug (Van Baerlestraat over the Vondelpark) are fine examples of this carved relative of the bridge letter.

*"Whenever I see Rondo being used I can't help but remember with sadness that its designer died in Auschwitz in 1944"*

Moving on to the area around Centraal station, take a stroll down Haarlemmerstraat and its continuation Haarlemmerdijk. It's a pleasant walk along a retail strip, which grows more charming the further west you walk. If you pay close attention to the façades you'll find some intriguing examples of gothic (132 Haarlemmerstraat) and art nouveau (51 Haarlemmerstraat; 39 Haarlemmerdijk) signs painted on coloured tiles.

At 82 Haarlemmerstraat there is a hardware and paint shop called Evert Bruijnesteijn BV. Its logo is set in the typeface Rondo, originally designed by Stefan Schlesinger for the Tetterode Foundry. During the second half of the 20th century it was a popular font and can still be found in the branding of several Dutch companies. Whenever I see Rondo being used I can't help but remember with sadness that Schlesinger died in Auschwitz in 1944.

If you get as far as the Binnen Oranjestraat it's just a 15-minute walk to one of Amsterdam's most beautiful neighbourhoods: Jordaan. Once you're there I encourage you to pay attention to the centuries-old façades and look for the traditional Dutch *gevelstenen* (gable stones). These stone tablets (*see page 120*) emerged in the 16th century before house numbers came into use. *Gevelstenen* usually combine an image with a sentence or motto related to the profession of the person at that address. Although they didn't use a single typeface, many inscriptions share common features. Most employ a roman all-caps font with pointed angles and a strong character, which I find very handsome.

To end this typographic walk – considering that you're already in the Jordaan district – I advise you to seek out some examples of Amsterdam's pub lettering called the Amsterdamse Krulletter (*see page 121*). This decorative, curvy script was created in the mid-20th century by Jan Willem Joseph Visser, a sign-painter who used to work for the Amstel brewery.

Visser was inspired by the work of the Dutch Golden Age's calligraphy masters. As his style became popular among bar owners it was painted on the windows of dozens of Amsterdam pubs, becoming an important element of the old *bruin* café (brown café) aesthetic. The homely cafés Hegeraad (34 Noordermarkt), Chris (42 Bloemstraat), De Nieuwe Lelie (83 Nieuwe Leliestraat) and Rooie Nelis (101 Laurierstraat) are good starting points.

Settle into a cosy window spot in one of these cafés, order a glass of *genever* and stare out at the hand-painted letters. Soon you'll find that while sipping the fragrant liquor in front of the arching lettering, you'll catch a glimpse of an old Amsterdam that stubbornly resists the passage of time. — (M)

**Best 'bruine' cafés with Krulletters**

**01 Café de Eland**
Cosy and quiet.
**02 Café 't Molentje**
Wood-panelled pub with live music.
**03 Café de Twee Zwaantjes**
Venerated staple known for folk singalongs.

ABOUT THE WRITER: Ramiro Espinoza specialised in type design at KABK in The Hague and the Plantin Institute of Typography in Antwerp. As well as contributing to design magazines he also runs the ReType Foundry, where he sells his own typefaces.

ESSAY 11

# After dark
## *The night manager*

———

Thanks to a little foresight and a creative approach, Amsterdammers have found a way to bridge their city's daytime and night-time economies.

*by Mirik Milan, night mayor*

Amsterdam is such a liveable city. The rent is relatively low, the culture offering is unmatched (we have more museums per square mileage than any other city) and the nightlife is better than ever. My position as night mayor started as a voluntary one in 2012 but the role was first introduced in 2003 when new legislation to restrict pole dancing was introduced by city hall. There was public and commercial outcry over the disconnect between politicians and the people: it was their city and if politicians had no clue about what was going on in late-night culture then they shouldn't be introducing prohibitive laws about it.

That was the first time that left-wing politicians decided they needed someone to inform them about what was going on at night. The first night mayor was appointed and they began the night watch, writing a manifesto about the relationship between the night-time economy and culture. The idea was born in the Netherlands and Amsterdam was the first city to ensure that the night mayor wasn't just a title but a position that catalysed positive change for the city.

Today we are an independent NGO with a budget between €50,000 and €60,00 per year and a team of 20. This includes 12 advisers from different backgrounds such as clubs, festivals, culture and diversity, as well as safety and regulations. Our approach is to first find the vision and then influence legislation. A lot of people don't realise how big the industry that operates between 20.00 and 08.00 is. When you look at the electronic-music industry alone in the Netherlands, it has an annual turnover of €600m and creates 13,000 jobs.

On top of that, you have the immeasurable aspect of the culture: there is a lot of talent development happening in the nightlife industry. Elizabeth Currid wrote a book called *The Warhol Economy: How Fashion, Art, and Music Drive New York City* and this is precisely how I see nightlife in Amsterdam. The night is the time for the unexpected and a place to create. But if you want to explain this to policymakers you have to speak their language; this is why we call ourselves rebels in suits. We need to have both industry and city hall working together to make smart policy.

The most influential policy change we've helped create over the years is the introduction of 24-hour venues: there are

---

**Legendary club venues**

———

**01 Melkweg**
Dates back to the 1970s and one of the few open until 05.00.
**02 Warehouse**
A seminal hardcore venue (formerly Elementenstraat).
**03 Gashouder**
Large-scale raves in an old gas reserve.

now 10 clubs and bars across the city with a 24-hour licence. Venues such as De School, Radion and Shelter are multidisciplinary, with a bar, restaurant, gallery and work space for young creatives, as well as a nightclub, which all help fund other cultural endeavours. This, in turn, encourages a shared responsibility for the space. Although these sites may be a little way out, Amsterdammers deem it worth cycling 25 minutes to get there.

Amsterdam definitely has its own personality. It's a small city so it's possible to experience many great things all in one night. In the future I'd love to see contemporary art and late-night culture become more integrated. I think it could be fantastic for all 60 museums here to develop a strong relationship with 60 nightclubs. Although I won't be night mayor forever, my life goal is to elevate the quality of nightlife to the point where the royal ballet could be connected to an electronic-music show and that would be your night out.

The night is when our creative people meet and draw inspiration from each other and I know it's not for everybody. But in Amsterdam the scene is brimming with proactive, open-minded, forward-thinking people who have different opinions on diversity and inclusivity. I think society could learn a lot from what happens in our city after dark. — (M)

ABOUT THE WRITER: Mirik Milan has worked as a club promoter, creative director and since 2012 as night mayor of Amsterdam. He's the capital's spokesman for all things nightlife and has successfully built a bridge between municipality, business owners and residents.

ESSAY 12
## Full circle
*Dutch food gets a makeover*

Worried you'll go hungry for quality food in Amsterdam? Today there's something for everyone in this diverse city – including excellent local fare – but it's true that this hasn't always been the case.

*by Vicky Hampton, food writer*

History is said to be cyclical and the story of the Netherlands' cuisine is no exception. While the Dutch Golden Age brought a bounty of exotic spices and fruit to the country from across its extensive empire, the 20th century saw a return to the simple diet of potatoes, cheap cuts of meat, fish and local vegetables that Amsterdammers had previously been used to. It's not for nothing that the Dutch are known for their frugality; being thrifty has proven useful in many aspects of life (very few Dutch have credit card debt) but it doesn't do much for the reputation of the national cuisine.

So it's not overly surprising that when I moved to Amsterdam from the UK in 2006, I fell in love with the city but not with its food. Lacking a national identity for its cuisine that didn't extend much beyond chips with mayo and the rather unidentifiable filling inside *bitterballen*, restaurants had turned to France for their inspiration. In the mid-2000s almost all the best examples served classic French cuisine, with a handful of decent Italian restaurants thrown in the mix. Dutch institutions such as Greetje were (and still are) offering traditional Lowlands' cuisine but, despite doing it rather well, there was hardly a broad appetite for the hearty and strangely named dishes: "pigeon's hangover", anyone?

Then something changed. As Amsterdam's chefs started to travel, the city's restaurant scene became as diverse as its visitors. Today diners can enjoy everything from Japanese *kaiseki* to Mexican tacos and Ethiopian *injera*. French fare fell out of fashion and Dutch chefs looked further and further afield for inspiration. I could pen an entire book about the diversity of cuisine in a city that calls itself home to more nationalities than any other metropolis on the planet (yes, including London and New York) but this is about the cycle of history, so I'll stick to topic.

True to form, more than a decade later we've come full circle once again: French food is back in vogue. Top chef Ron Blaauw, known for being on the cutting edge of culinary trends, opened Ron Gastrobar Paris in 2016. It's a buzzing bistro-style restaurant that transports you straight to the City of Light with its retro *oeufs* mimosa and steak tartare. Meanwhile, Auberge Jean & Marie has opened in the hip De Pijp area, proving that fine wine and frogs' legs are popular even among millennials (at least, those who can afford them).

But more important still is the positive turn that Dutch food itself has taken. In some cases this applies only to the ingredients; in others it applies to the style of cooking. Many Dutch chefs (just like most chefs worldwide) have long been of the opinion that the closer the provenance of the produce, the better-tasting the dish. Which is why restaurant De Kas (*see page 35*), housed in a greenhouse that produces the majority of the vegetables, fruit and herbs used

*"Dutch institutions like Greetje were offering traditional cuisine but there was hardly a broad appetite for the strangely named dishes: 'pigeon's hangover', anyone?"*

in its kitchen, has already stood the test of time for more than a decade. Likewise, Marius has been serving a "market menu" of four fixed courses, depending on what's fresh and in season at the market, since the early 2000s.

Newer restaurants in Amsterdam have taken things one step further. Guts & Glory (*see page 27*) uses a related concept in which the menu focuses on chapters (an animal, for example, or a particular cuisine) that change every couple of months. In the east of the city, Eetbar Wilde Zwijnen has been serving small sharing plates of modern Dutch seasonal fare, such as lamb belly and white asparagus, since 2015.

Two restaurants, however, have really raised the stakes. Choux (*see page 36*) is nestled under the railway line close to Centraal station; one look at the menu shows how serious chef Merijn van Berlo is about Dutch produce. *Stoofpeer* (spiced, stewed Gieser Wildeman pears) and *zuurkool* (Holland's answer to sauerkraut) feature in one dish. *Monniksbaard* (a succulent plant that grows in salty coastal areas) and shellfish feature in another. The wine selection is equally interesting. While they may not be Dutch (wine is produced in the south of the country but tends to be expensive for the level of quality), they are organic.

Meanwhile, Restaurant Breda (named after a small city in the country's south) knocked the socks off Amsterdam's food scene in 2016. A simple plate of charred runner beans with a mint purée took me straight back to my parents' garden when I was a child. The refined yet elegant flavours continued throughout the five-course dinner, right through to the sorrel granita, which was grassy and spiked with ginger. Traditional Dutch food it is not but Breda is bringing back local ingredients within an international context – and making it work spectacularly.

A decade after moving to Amsterdam I can honestly say that I'm now as enamoured with its cuisine as I was with its canals all those years ago. I'm curious about what the next decade has in store; I can only hope that we're about to enter the Golden Age of Dutch cuisine. — (M)

---

**Picks for
dining out**

**01 Choux**
Locally sourced food and
organic wine.
**02 Breda**
Creative, accomplished and
modern Dutch cooking.
**03 Eetbar Wilde Zwijnen**
Small sharing plates of
Dutch fare.

ABOUT THE WRITER: Vicky Hampton is a British-born food writer who's been living in Amsterdam since 2006. She runs the website *amsterdamfoodie.nl* and writes for several publications and guidebooks. She recently applied for Dutch citizenship.

# Culture
——— Dutch mastery

With thousands of exhibits packed within its walls, the Rijksmuseum alone has enough cultural riches to make a capital city blush. That it's just one of Amsterdam's jewels means you'll never be far from somewhere enchanting to explore.

The city's art history is something to be proud of and investment has built new museums and given facelifts to others. But if you fancy sidestepping the crowds swarming around the Old Masters there's a vibrant modern-art scene to explore outside the Museumplein. In this section we list the small galleries, photography studios and modern-art houses leading the way.

Amsterdam's liberal reputation is well known and that rebellious streak is apparent in its small theatres, cutting-edge art projects, eclectic music venues and independent cinemas. We'll direct you to the best, as well as to free classical concerts at Het Concertgebouw. The 17th century may have been the Golden Age but culturally the capital is still shining bright.

**Museums**
Art and artefacts

① Rijksmuseum, Oud-Zuid
*The full monty*

What will you see when visiting the Rijksmuseum? Oh, you know: sculptures from the Middle Ages; 18th-century decorative arts; a bit of everything from the 19th century; 20th-century minimalism and modernism; the zero movement; romanesques; the baroque; mannerism; gothic art; the renaissance; rococo; classicism; the Italianate; art nouveau; impressionism; Romanticism; bronzes; still lifes; Asian art; artefacts from 11th-century churches; Vermeer; Van Gogh; Rembrandt; silverware; Samurai helmets; ceremonial swords; Meissen porcelain; Delft pottery; a tiny potty; a lead-booted diving suit; models of ships; lighthouses; and shoes.

"Less is more," says director Taco Dibbits. Less? There are about 8,000 objects in 80 galleries chosen from one million pieces in the collection. "It was really a case of 'kill your darlings'," he says of the choice. Luckily, he still has 992,000 darlings left to play with.
*1 Museumstraat, 1071 XX*
*+ 31 (0)20 674 7000*
*rijksmuseum.nl*

② 
Stedelijk Museum, Oud-Zuid
*Make it modern*

The Stedelijk Museum has been
a central part of the city's cultural
landscape since 1874. Its curation
focuses on contemporary and
modern art (primarily from the
1920s and onwards) and shows big
names such as Chagall, Rothko and
Lichtenstein, as well as up-and-
coming artists.

Two major renovations have
given room to allow the gallery's
scope to expand. These include
the 2012 "bathtub" extension and
the 1950s wing, which was built
to house works from Amsterdam-
based artists.
*10 Museumplein, 1071 DJ*
*+31 (0)20 573 2911*
*stedelijk.nl*

**De Stijl movement**

The distinct primary-colour
patchwork of the De Stijl
movement has its origins
in the Netherlands. Dutch
painters Theo van Doesburg
and Piet Mondrian founded
the publication *De Stijl*
(meaning *The Style*) in 1917 as
a mouthpiece for their ideas
on art and utopian society. It
led to the abstract movement,
with its use of vertical and
horizontal geometry.

The movement's reach
extended to literature, music,
typography, industrial design
and most notably architecture
with the rise of the International
Style in the 1920s and 1930s.

In 2017 the Stedelijk
Museum marked De Stijl's
100-year anniversary with a
major retrospective. There is
also a permanent exhibition.

③
Van Gogh Museum, Oud-Zuid
*A masterpiece for masterpieces*

This is one of the most visited
galleries in the world so battling
crowds is inevitable. The museum
houses the largest collection of the
Dutch post-impressionist painter's
work, including "Sunflowers",
"Almond Blossom", "The
Bedroom" and "Potato Eaters".

A new entrance designed by
Dutch architect Hans van Heeswijk
was added in 2015 to help with
the flow of people. It sits in stark
contrast to Gerrit Rietveld's 1973
De Stijl-inspired original.
*6 Museumplein, 1071 DJ*
*+31 (0)20 570 5200*
*vangoghmuseum.nl*

## ④
### Eye Filmmuseum, Noord
*Movie buff heaven*

In 2012 the Filmmuseum relocated from Vondelpark to its new distinctive home on the IJ harbourfront, directly opposite Centraal station. Dusting off its collection dedicated to the world of film, it's now a modern shrine for silver-screen aficionados. "We want to show a wide spectrum of the art of film, including great retrospectives from Kubrick to Fellini but also more obscure and experimental work," says Sandra den Hamer, director of Eye. The exhibitions are shown in the versatile and expansive space and the cinema's four screens offer a mix of avant garde and arthouse films, Dutch classics and Hollywood blockbusters.

The wide-ranging programme also includes weekly series such as *Eye On Art*, a partnership with the city's top galleries, and cinema concerts, presenting silent films with live music. The building is home to a top-notch gift shop, selling everything from vintage film posters (*see page 66*) to Lolita sunglasses and wine from Francis Ford Coppola's vineyard. There's also a restaurant and bar.
*1 IJpromenade, 1031 KT*
*+ 31 (0)20 589 1400*
*eyefilm.nl*

## ①
### Kunstverein, Jordaan
*Experimental art*

Toronto-born Maxine Kopsa co-founded Kunstverein in 2009 as a platform for artists she considered to be historically overlooked. The intimate space is near the bigger commercial galleries in Jordaan but has a more distinctive and experimental tone. Kunstverein's roster of lectures, screenings and performances doesn't follow the traditional format: exhibitions are rarely limited to pictures on walls, instead often spilling over into books and sometimes furniture.

Previous shows have featured works from Israeli choreographer Noa Eshkol and British constructivism maverick Marlow Moss. The gallery also has an independent publishing arm and sells print publications that will appeal to graphic-design enthusiasts and offbeat-art lovers.
*28 Hazenstraat, 1016 SR*
*+ 31 (0)20 331 3203*
*kunstverein.nl*

## ②
### Huis Marseille, Centrum
*Quiet location*

Amsterdam's first photography museum opened its doors in 1999 in a unique setting. Huis Marseille's two 17th-century canal houses might not look much from the outside but hiding within are a library, garden and photo exhibitions hung in two princely Golden Age-era rooms.

Less crowded and more serene than Fotografiemuseum Amsterdam (Foam), this is a better option for exploring high-quality photographs in great detail. The gallery closes one week before all new exhibitions so be sure to check.
*401 Keizersgracht, 1016 EK*
*+ 31 (0)20 531 8989*
*huismarseille.nl*

**④**

Pakt, Eastern Docklands
*Emerging talent*

Art historian Nienke Vijlbrief and artist Rob van de Werdt decided to join forces in 2003 and create a space to give art-academy graduates and emerging talent a platform. At the time, surging rents in the city were causing artists to depart for Rotterdam and Berlin so local government began offering affordable studio space, which the pair snapped up.

"We think it's important for younger artists to be given the means, space and time to develop and show new work," says Vijlbrief. "Pakt functions as a bridge between art academies, artist-run initiatives and the established galleries and museums." It's housed in a warehouse in the Eastern Docklands area, which is experiencing steady regeneration. The duo look for artists who fully explore the capacity of the space.
*53 Zeeburgerpad, 1019 AB*
*+31 (0)6 5427 0879*
*pakt.nu*

**③**

W139, Centrum
*Risky business*

In 1979 young artists Guus van der Werf, Marianne Kronenberg, Martha Crijns, Reinout Weydom and Ad de Jong transformed an old theatre in the red-light district into an anti-establishment space to show their works to friends. By 1990 it was a bona fide gallery with a motto of "room for risk".

Today W139 remains an artist-run gallery with a rebellious streak. Its exhibitions, which feature both Dutch and international talent, may be too out-there for some but for hardcore art fans it's a window into 1980s Amsterdam counterculture.
*139 Warmoesstraat, 1012 JB*
*+31 (0)20 622 9434*
*w139.nl*

**Out of town**

Following funding problems, De Appel, one of the city's best curators of contemporary art, moved out of the city centre to Westlandgracht. It's worth the journey as exhibitions here rarely disappoint and the graduates it champions often go on to achieve great things.
*deappel.nl*

### ① Grimm, Centrum
*Twice as good*

Showing contemporary art since 2005, Jorg Grimm's gallery has rapidly gained a reputation on the global art stage. His roster of increasingly international artists has included Charles Avery, Matthew Day Jackson and Daniel Richter.

Since 2010 Grimm has been based on the pretty Frans Halsstraat in De Pijp and in 2017 opened a second space in De 9 Straatjes. Both the industrial space in De Pijp and the charming 17th-century canal house complement the vast range of exhibited work.
*26 Frans Halsstraat, 1072 BR;*
*241 Keizersgracht, 1016 EA*
*+31 (0)20 675 2465*
*grimmgallery.com*

### ② Annet Gelink Gallery, Jordaan
*Making a point*

There's a cluster of commercial galleries in the south of Jordaan, where Annet Gelink Gallery has been since 2000. Founder Annet Gelink and director Floor Wullems have built a stable of talent, mostly discovered at the Rijksakademie.

Represented artists include Amsterdam resident Maria Barnas, Japanese film director Meiro Koizumi and Israeli artist Yael Bartana; there's also Croatian David Maljkovic, who explores the cultural and social heritage of his home country. The gallery's oeuvre is hard-hitting and often political.
*187-189 Laurierstraat, 1016 PL*
*+31 (0)20 330 2066*
*annetgelink.com*

③
Ellen de Bruijne Projects, Jordaan
*Cutting-edge artists*

Hidden among Jordaan's many
galleries you'll find a discreet
door buzzer between shops on
the Rozengracht high street. This
is Ellen de Bruijne Projects, which
opened in 1999 with a rebellious
social and subtly feminist voice.
Over the years it has resisted the
pull of the mainstream and still
feels in tune with the innovative
subculture of the city.

Still-life photographer and
Amsterdam resident Uta Eisenreich,
and Bulgarian performance artist
Zhana Ivanova, are among its roll
call of conceptual artists.
*207A Rozengracht, 1016 LZ*
*+ 31 (0)20 530 4994*
*edbprojects.com*

④
Galerie Juliètte Jongma, De Pijp
*Leading the way*

In many respects, Galerie Juliètte
Jongma is a trailblazer. It opened
in De Pijp in 2004, long before it
was cool to do so. Galleries such
as Grimm (*see page 95*) have since
followed, creating a contemporary-
art hub south of the canal ring.

The roster of artists here
includes Armenian sculptor Karen
Sargsyan, Dutch film-maker Guido
van der Werve and US painter and
print-maker Melissa Gordon, who
were all spotted by Jongma at the
beginning of their careers. With
about seven shows a year, there's
always something new.
*128A Gerard Doustraat, 1073 VX*
*+ 31 (0)20 463 6904*
*juliettejongma.com*

*Apologies if we're
looking a bit miffed*

**5**

Galerie Fons Welters, Jordaan
*The godfather*

As one of the oldest and arguably the most powerful, Fons Welters is the grandfather of commercial galleries and one whose eccentric house is always worth a visit. Art wasn't the obvious career path for him: he started out helping on his father's farm before moving to the bright lights in the riotous 1980s.

For more than three decades his gallery has grown on the national and international stages and helped shape the commercial offerings in the city. Welters has a particular knack for finding compelling sculpture and installation artists.
*140 Bloemstraat, 1016 LJ*
*+31 (0)20 423 3046*
*fonswelters.nl*

**Off-the-wall offerings**
Weird and wonderful

**1**

De School, De Baarsjes
*Independent venue*

This multi-use space comes from the team behind Trouw, an iconic venue in an old printing factory that closed in 2015. "When we were looking for a site we cycled around looking for somewhere that we could give a new dimension to," says managing director Ernst Mertens.

When the team came across a former technical college they knew they'd found their location; they turned it into a club, restaurant, art space and gym in 2016. All of the programming is independently curated so it remains current.
*1 Doctor Jan van Breemenstraat, 1056 AB*
*+31 (0)20 737 3197*
*deschoolamsterdam.nl*

**Give it a go**

There's no permanent address for Eddie The Eagle Museum but this artist-run collective drums up bizarre and brilliant content. Named after the UK ski jumper, it's about the art of trying, from performance through to photography.
*eddietheeaglemuseum.com*

**②**
Pakhuis de Zwijger, Eastern
Docklands
*Talking shop*

Pakhuis de Zwijger opened in
2006 in a modernist warehouse in
Eastern Docklands. The not-for-
profit organisation hosts debates,
discussions and think-tanks on
everything from quality of life,
innovation and technology to
the relationship between the
government and citizens.

Talks are usually in Dutch but
some are in English depending
on the guests and topics covered.
With more than 600 events
annually, it's a dynamic place to
drop by to engage in a lively chat.
*179 Piet Heinkade, 1019 HC*
*+ 31 (0)20 624 6380*
*dezwijger.nl*

**Live venues**
Face the action

**①**
Muziekgebouw aan 't IJ and
Bimhuis, Eastern Docklands
*Moving music*

Two of the Netherlands' best
music venues reside side by side.
The award-winning buildings
by Danish firm 3XN are home to
contemporary and classical-music
hall the Muziekgebouw aan 't IJ
and Bimhuis, the place for jazz.

Muziekgebouw has movable
walls, floors and ceilings that adapt
to suit musical styles, while the
Bimhuis's amphitheatre hall is
more intimate.
*Muziekgebouw aan 't IJ:*
*1 Piet Heinkade, 1019 BR*
*+31 (0)20 788 2000; muziekgebouw.nl*
*Bimhuis:*
*3 Piet Heinkade, 1019 BR*
*+31 (0)20 788 1250; bimhuis.nl*

## ② Het Concertgebouw, Oud-Zuid
*Top of the classical*

Since hosting its first concert in 1888, this Amsterdam institution has become one of the world's most respected halls: Gustav Mahler, Richard Strauss, Louis Armstrong and Cecilia Bartoli have all graced its stage. You can watch a symphonic orchestra in the majestic Main Hall, opt for chamber music in the Recital Hall or settle in the intimate Choir Hall. Even if you're not a seasoned enthusiast, it's worth a visit. On Wednesdays the Concertgebouw hosts free lunchtime concerts.
*10 Concertgebouwplein, 1071 LN*
*+31 (0)20 573 0573*
*concertgebouw.nl*

## ③ Paradiso, Centrum
*Young at heart*

Known for its eclectic mix of shows, Paradiso is a musical mainstay on the edge of the canal ring. A converted church dating back to the 19th century, it opened its doors as a music venue in 1968.

Since then it's been a centre for counter and youth culture. From punk in the 1970s to raves in the 1990s, acts such as The Cure, The Roots, Amy Winehouse and Lenny Kravitz have all performed here. Paradiso also hosts wider cultural projects such as fashion shows, film screenings and lectures.
*6-8 Weteringschans, 1017 SG*
*+31 (0)20 626 4521*
*paradiso.nl*

## ④ Frascati Theater, Centrum
*Acting up*

The Frascati Theater dates back to the 1580s when it was a haunt for intellectuals in the bustling trade district. Its name came later, from a coffeehouse that opened within the venue in 1810. A 1,500-capacity ballroom was added, drawing in audiences for live vaudeville comedies and kickstarting the area's entertainment scene.

Today the Frascati has four theatre spaces: three at 63 Nes and another at 71 Nes. It's a centre for live performance, hosts more than 700 shows annually and is a breeding ground for new talent.
*63 Nes, 1012 KD*
*+31 (0)20 626 6866*
*frascatitheater.nl*

① 
Filmtheater De Uitkijk, Centrum
*Cinematic heritage*

When De Uitkijk opened in 1912,
moviegoers would buy their tickets
from a booth outside before
entering the single-screen theatre.
A café and foyer have been added
but you can still see the original
ticket machine on display.

Entrepreneur Bart Lubbers
bought the cinema in 2007
and placed its programming in
the hands of the same student
organisation that looks after
Kriterion (*see page 102*). A mainly
European bill offers themed
seasons, wine evenings and silent
films with live music.
*452 Prinsengracht, 1017 KE*
*+ 31 (0)20 223 2416*
*uitkijk.nl*

**Amsterdam on film**

**01** Diamonds Are Forever,
1971: Amsterdam makes
a cameo in the sixth and
last James Bond film to
star Sean Connery when
tourists on a boat witness
a body being pulled from
the Amstel River near the
Magere Brug. Be sure to
note Bond's mistake: the
secret agent, disguised
as a Dutch diamond
smuggler, greets his
enemy with the German
"*Guten abend*" instead of
the Dutch "*Goedenavond*".

**02** Turkish Delight, 1973:
Directed by Paul
Verhoeven, this turbulent
love story, based on the
erotic 1969 novel by Jan
Wolkers, received an
Oscar nomination for best
foreign-language film. Set
within the bohemian art
world in Amsterdam, it
is a raw depiction of a
turbulent love story.

**03** Amsterdamned, 1988:
This Dutch cult horror film
directed by Dick Maas
turns Amsterdam's historic
canal ring into a hellish
nightmare. After several
bodies are found floating
in the city's waterways,
a detective discovers
something sinister lurking
beneath the surface.

**04** Black Book, 2006: Two
decades after leaving the
Netherlands, renowned
director Paul Verhoeven
(*see above*) returned from
Hollywood to make this
big-budget thriller. Based
on true events, it tells the
story of a young Jewish
woman who becomes a
spy for the resistance
during the Second World
War. Pivotal scenes were
shot in Amsterdam; at the
time of its release it was
the most expensive Dutch
film ever made.

**2**

Tuschinski, Centrum
*Ornate beauty*

Polish businessman Abraham Icek Tuschinski first became mesmerised by the silver screen after designing the uniforms for cinema porters. Not long after, he commissioned the construction of a spate of film theatres across the Netherlands, the most prominent of which was his eponymous masterpiece in the capital. Doors opened in 1921 and the interior design combined a beautiful mix of Amsterdam School, art nouveau and art deco styles.

Painstakingly preserved and now owned by Pathé, the Tuschinski is still considered one of Europe's most ornate and decadent cinemas. The main 740-seat auditorium plays the blockbusters while the five smaller theatres show a more independent roster. To soak up the full rich history, ask about the audio tour.
*26-28 Reguliersbreestraat, 1017 CN pathe.nl*

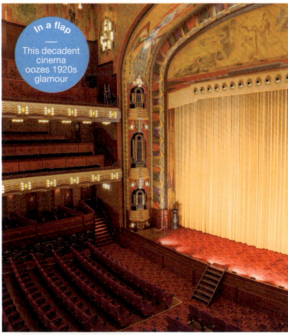

**In a flap**
—
This decadent cinema oozes 1920s glamour

*The gallery gave me a right earful for doing this*

The Movies, Jordaan
*History maker*

Like Filmtheater De Uitkijk
(*see page 100*), The Movies began
screening in 1912, making it one
of the oldest cinemas in town (it's
rumoured that the original art deco
interior inspired Tuschinski). It
started off with a single screen but
in 1971 the owners acquired space
in the neighbouring buildings and
expanded to four screening rooms.

   In 1989 another room was
added, along with a restaurant next
to the entrance. The programming
now finds a happy medium
between blockbuster and arthouse.
*161 Haarlemmerdijk, 1013 KH*
*+31 (0)20 638 6016*
*themovies.nl*

**3**
Kriterion, De Plantage
*Student beginnings*

This former Jewish workers' union
building was transformed into a
cinema by a group of students in
1945. During the Second World
War they were actively involved
in the resistance movements
and afterwards they founded the
Kriterion as a way of supporting
other students, employing them
to make studies more affordable.

   Kriterion is still student-run and
at the countercultural heart of the
city. It shows edgy arthouse films,
eclectic documentaries and Oscar
winners. The café charges are
modest and it hosts live music.
*170 Roetersstraat, 1018 WE*
*+31 (0)20 623 1708*
*kriterion.nl*

## ②
### Athenaeum Nieuwscentrum, Centrum
*Alternative newsstand*

Kiosk culture isn't big in the city; instead newsstands tend to come in the form of bookshop-kiosks. The Nieuwscentrum at the Athenaeum Boekhandel, the Netherlands' biggest independent bookshop (see page 62), is the city's best-known spot for buying the latest copies of your favourite publications. It stocks international magazines covering everything from current affairs to art, fashion and cooking. The staff are happy to share their knowledge about anything going on in the world of print.
*14 Spui, 1012 RM*
*+31 (0)20 514 1470*
*athenaeum.nl*

### ①
### Magazines, citywide
*The printed word*

Amsterdam's independent magazine and newspaper scene is thriving. ❶ *De Volkskrant* is a quality national daily; for a slightly more left-leaning read, ❷ *Het Parool* is the most popular local newspaper and was named European newspaper of the year in 2016 (it's a daily that's published in the afternoon). For in-depth analysis of current affairs look to ❸ *De Groene Amsterdammer.* It's the Netherlands' esteemed left-leaning magazine with thought-provoking articles on society; it has an aesthetic similar to that of *The New Yorker.*

A range of insightful English-language publications have also hit newsstands in recent years. Pick up a copy of ❹ *MacGuffin*, the winner of the magazine-of-the-year award at the 2016 Stack Awards, to find out about the life of ordinary objects (such as a window, rope or sink,) and stories about their purpose and design.

❺ *Mark* focuses on modern architecture, covering "starchitects to new talent alike". The team behind it also publish ❻ *Frame*: a leading publication about interior design that covers everything from retail spaces to offices.

The conceptual photography magazine ❼ *Ordinary* explores one seemingly mundane object per issue but asks artists to send in their "extraordinary" take on the object. ❽ *Voortuin* is an interesting example of artist-run experimental publishing.

### Monocle 24

It would be remiss not to mention Monocle's own radio station, which features programmes ranging from daily news to our design show *Section D*. Listen online at *monocle.com/radio* or download the podcasts on iTunes or SoundCloud.

### Radio

**01 Red Light Radio:** This online station playing international music broadcasts from the heart of the red-light district – a window onto Oudekerksplein allows passers-by to peer in. It was founded in 2010 and was awarded the Mixcloud Best Online Radio Station in 2015.
*redlightradio.net*

**02 BNR:** For opinion and reportage on political, business and financial news while in the capital, tune into Business Nieuws Radio on wavelength 101.8 FM. All the programming is in Dutch.
*bnr.nl*

**03 Salto:** This open-access broadcaster is run out of the same building as Pakhuis de Zwijger (see page 98) and offers seven different stations including WereldFM, which often has English-language programming.
*salto.nl*

# Design and architecture
—— Sites to behold

Amsterdam's architecture dates back to the 14th century and when you imagine the city it's hard not to think solely in terms of canals, bridges and windmills. But the scope of design in the Dutch capital is wider and more diverse than the postcards might have you believe.

The brick-heavy work of the Amsterdam School, as espoused by Eduard Cuypers and his acolytes, is of particular interest, blending expressionism with art deco and art nouveau. At the same time, members of the movement were careful to apply socialist ideals that buildings should benefit all, not just the elite.

A respect for the city's architectural history has also led to the repurposing of structures that would otherwise have lain idle, themselves becoming a symbol of the city's pleasing juxtaposition of old and new. And there's plenty of modern and contemporary design to catch the eye too, from brutalist accommodation blocks to innovative solutions to the city's housing shortage.

**Amphibious architecture**
High and dry

① 
REM Eiland, Noord
*Rigged up as a restaurant*

**Food channel**
——
The original studio is now a private dining area

Standing on 12-metre-tall stilts, the red-and-white chequered REM Eiland was erected in 1964 and then towed 9km offshore into the North Sea where it was anchored to the seabed. Its purpose was to house the pirate broadcasting station Radio and TV Noordzee but after government objections the station was dismantled by the Royal Dutch Navy a few months later. It eventually resumed broadcast as a legal station and was on air until 2006, when it was again dismantled.

In 2011 the boxy three-storey structure took up a new residence in the IJ harbour just north of the city and opened as a restaurant. It still features the original footbridges, signal lights and lifeboat, while the former helipad is now a terrace offering great (if windswept) views back over the city from ust over 20 metres up.
*45-2 Haparandadam, 1013 AK*
*+31 (0)20 688 5501*
*remeiland.com*

**2**
Silodam, Centrum
*Housing block*

Silodam was inspired by the 19th and 20th-century grain silos on the docks of Oude Houthaven just to the northwest of Centraal station. In 1995 Rotterdam-based studio MVRDV – also responsible for the Chanel shop (*see page 80*) and Tennisclub IJburg (*see page 124*) – was commissioned to design a dense living complex in the empty port. Finished in 2003, the monumental building looks like a stack of shipping containers servicing the surrounding silos.

The site houses 165 commercial and residential units of varying sizes, occupied by a cross-section of financial categories (and also, therefore, of Amsterdam's society). MVRDV created internal streets and central shared spaces, including a restaurant, library and viewing deck. There's also a small harbour for residents to moor their boats. Tours can be booked in advance.
*Silodam, 1013 AW*
*silodam.org*

**3**
Kraanspoor, Noord
*Glazed look*

Dreamed up by Trude Hooykaas, founder of OTH Architecten, on a bicycle ride (how very Dutch) in 1997, Kraanspoor faced numerous roadblocks, including objections from city hall. The 270-metre-long glass office building took a decade to complete and appears to float three metres above a decommissioned crane track on the IJ river.

Hooykaas wanted to preserve the area's industrial heritage while giving it a new lease on life. The building's façade is a wraparound transparent second skin of movable glass louvres that afford spectacular views of the IJ river.
*Kraanspoor, 1033 SE*

**4**
Steigereiland, IJburg
*Floating houses*

With the city's housing shortage, architects have been looking to the water, developing practical but good-looking floating homes. Nearly 75 of them now dot the artificial island cluster of IJburg in the city's east. A network of aluminium-surfaced jetties work as footpaths and create a link between the two and three-storey dwellings, which range from social housing to high-end abodes.

One cluster was designed by Marlies Rohmer Architects, using glass and synthetic materials that resemble steel. The base is a hollow cement cube, which is poured in one go and takes into consideration heavy pieces of furniture such as pianos or bathtubs (a thicker slab of concrete on the opposite side acts as a counterweight). Once finished, the houses are pulled along the canals by barge to their destination.
*Haringbuisdijk, 1086 VA*
*rohmer.nl*

**Old meets new**
Updated greats

### ① Canteen Building, Eastern Docklands
*Lofty ideals*

As the name suggests, this was once the canteen building for the now defunct Royal Dutch Steamboat Company – but new life was breathed into the site in the early 1990s. The city council divided the original space into eight loft apartments, which it sold off for symbolic sums to artist squatters.

"We used old ship ladders to provide an individual entrance for each loft," says Koen Crabbendam of Casa Architecten, who worked on the initial brief. The artists renovated the lofts themselves and owned the properties under the condition that they did not sell them for the first 10 years. Once the decade was up, some of the properties soon went for more than €1m.
*1-15 Levantplein, 1019 MA*

### ② Rijksmuseum, Oud-Zuid
*Refreshing the past*

Ten years of renovations to Pierre Cuypers' 1885 neo-gothic building were completed in 2013; the main hall is now an open courtyard by Seville architects Cruz and Ortiz. "There's so much light now, it's a whole different mentality," says gallery director Taco Dibbits. Teams dug beneath sea level to find more space and height for the glass-roofed courtyard. "In the Netherlands as soon as you put a spade in the ground you need a sailor, not a builder," adds Dibbits, referencing the trouble with building on reclaimed land.

Now a concave tier of Portuguese stone is overlooked by a pair of towering new minimalist porticos nudging up to the walls of Cuypers' outspoken original. The interior design, lighting and staging of works was refreshed by Frenchman Jean-Michel Wilmotte.
*1 Museumstraat, 1071 XX*
*+31 (0)20 674 7000*
*rijksmuseum.nl*

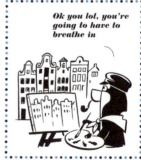

*Ok you lot, you're going to have to breathe in*

**③**
Gebouw 27E Marineterrein, Oost
*Military planning*

Dutch architecture bureau SLA
was tasked with transforming this
former military academy into
a setting fit to host the EU Council
during the Netherlands' presidency
back in 2016. Before that, the
13-hectare marine base had been
closed for more than 300 years.

"There was a lot of mystery
surrounding this site, particularly
since it's right in the city centre,"
says Peter Van Assche, lead
designer at bureau SLA. The façade
was redesigned, each window
gaining oversized wooden louvres
abstractly representing European
flags. Spread out over three
floors, the building's large, open
spaces are now used as various
types of workspaces that are either
open to the public or rented out
to start-ups.
*Marineterrein, 5 Kattenburgerstraat,
1018 JA
+31 (0)20 261 3656
marineterrein.nl*

**④**
Het Scheepvaartmuseum,
Eastern Docklands
*Top of the charts*

Daniël Stalpaert, who also
designed the town hall (now the
royal palace), used his trademark
austere classical style for Het
Scheepvaartmuseum (The
National Maritime Museum). Built
as a naval warehouse in 1656, it
opened as a museum in 1973 and
was renovated from 2007 to 2011;
it was during this time that its
courtyard was roofed with 1,200
pieces of glass. The design was
inspired by compass lines on old
mapping charts, with LEDs placed
on each of the 868 "knots".
*1 Kattenburgerplein, 1018 KK
+31 (0)20 523 2222
hetscheepvaartmuseum.nl*

⑤
Stedelijk Museum, Oud-Zuid
*Added extras*

AW Weissman's Stedelijk Museum
was completed in the Dutch
neo-renaissance style in 1895 but
various additions have been made
to it over the years. The most
ambitious was finished in 2012 by
Benthem Crouwel Architects and
took the form of a large white-and-
glass wing known affectionately as
the *badkuip* (bathtub).

"We wanted our design to
include an urban-planning
solution," says Mels Crouwel,
founding partner at Benthem
Crouwel. To achieve this the team
reoriented the main entrance by
180 degrees to face Museumplein.
"In doing so it created an active,
common ground for the first time
between all the square's cultural
spaces," adds Crouwel.
*10 Museumplein, 1071 DJ*
*+31 (0)20 573 2911*
*stedelijk.nl*

**Residential**
Living legends

①
The Pyramids, Westerpark
*Three sides to every storey*

The Pyramids are the highlight of
Marcanti-eiland's redevelopment,
started in the 1980s. Finished in 2006
by Soeters van Eldonk Architecten,
these 50-metre-tall triangles imitate
the shape of the industrial district
and tap into HP Berlage's vision
of the Amsterdam School.

The towers take the form of
traditional gables, their stepped
sides doubling as terraces, and
house 82 apartments also designed
by Soeters van Eldonk. The
Pyramids' compact form allows for
a large square on the half-sunken
roof of an extensive garage, finished
with ventilation pipes inspired
by old-fashioned chimneys.
*Jan van Galenstraat, 1051 KE*

### De Oude Kerk

It may not be as grandiose as gothic cathedrals elsewhere but De Oude Kerk is nonetheless impressive (and also the oldest building in Amsterdam). Wood was the primary material used during construction to ensure that the foundation wouldn't overload and sink: a very real concern for a city built on peat swamps. The church was consecrated at the beginning of the 14th century and operated until 1951, when it was closed due to concerns about the integrity of the foundations.

Extensive restoration took place between 1955 and 1979,` and again between 1994 and 1998. Today Oude Kerk is home to an art institution that allows installation artists to create works that fit the soaring wooden ceilings and cracked stone floorspace. *oudekerk.nl*

② Nieuwendammerdijk, Noord
*Triumphs in timber*

These distinctive pretty houses, lining a long and narrow street in Noord, tell the history of a small village on the IJ river. They date back to the 16th century and were made of wood (unlike the typical Amsterdam stone canal houses) to ensure the dyke could hold their weight.

Constructed during the golden age of shipbuilding, trade and maritime transport, the embellished abodes were the homes of captains, fishermen, ferrymen and lock-keepers, not to mention wealthy families (number 202-204 was built for shipbuilding magnate de Vries Lentsch). The neoclassical houses at numbers 300 and 308 were home to doctor Johann Georg Mezger, one of the founders of physiotherapy. Princess Sophia of Nassau, wife of the Swedish prince and later King Oscar II, gave him land in Nieuwendam to thank him for treating her oldest son.
*Nieuwendammerdijk, 1023 BT*

### Tricks of the trade

Visit the Museum Van Loon to see how the merchants lived in the golden era of trade. The Van Loon family (of Dutch East-India Company descent) has lived here since 1884 and opened part of the residence in 1973 to share its private collection with the public. *museumvanloon.nl*

**3**

Betondorp, Oost
*Concrete craftsmanship*

This brutalist neighbourhood of 900 minimalist, art deco houses in the city's south was built in the 1920s as part of a construction experiment to address the country's rising brick prices and shortage of skilled workers. It was also a pilot project to determine the efficiency of varying low-cost building techniques for public housing.

Betondorp, which translates as "concrete village", was designed by a group of architects and construction companies to use 10 different concrete mixes. The layout roughly follows the self-contained communities of the garden-city movement, meaning the detached houses with private gardens are single-family dwellings centred around a communal square. Sitting next to this concrete cluster are an additional 1,000 homes built of brick and designed by architects Jan Gratama and Gerrit Versteeg.
*Brink, 1097 TW*

### Old school
In an attempt to combat tuberculosis before the Second World War, the Dutch government commissioned *openlichtscholen* (open-air schools). The first was Eerste Openluchtschool, located on Cliostraat, designed by Jan Duiker and completed in 1930.

**4**

Krom Boomssloot
warehouses, Centrum
*Lots in store*

The double warehouses of Krom
Boomssloot were originally home
to naval workers and located
in an industrial shipping area.
Shipbuilder and former city mayor
Cornelis Pietersz Boom owned
them, hence the name.

Some of the façades, wooden
shutters and courtyards have been
preserved from the 17th century
and are now national monuments.
Highlights include the 1980s art
initiative Schottenburch (numbers
18 to 20) and the Armenian
Apostolic church (number 22)
but most are now apartments
with hefty price tags.
*16-22 Krom Boomssloot, 1011 GW*

**5**

Oostelijk Havengebied,
Eastern Docklands
*Warehouse renovations*

The docklands' 19th-century
warehouses were replaced
with high-density residential
developments between the late
1980s and early 2000s. Tour them
on two-wheels, starting at the
eastern peninsulas of Borneo and
Sporenburg, which feature three-
storey houses by urban designers
West 8. Three sculptural blocks
(look out for The Whale) stand
in stark contrast to these low-rise
waterfront dwellings.

Cycle along Stokerkade, looking
across the canal to the diverse
houses on Scheepstimmermanstraat,
which were designed by their
owners. Jo Coenen, known for
Amsterdam's public library,
designed KNSM-eiland, where
large blocks flank a grand avenue
overlooking the IJ. End further west
on the adjacent Java-eiland with
Sjoerd Soeters' contemporary take
on the historic Dutch canal house.
*The Whale, 224 Baron GA, Tindalstraat*

## Amsterdam School
Prime movers

01

Between 1910 and 1930, the Amsterdam School movement dominated architecture in the city. However, architects who started out in the studio of Eduard Cuypers had been playing around with this style for a while: the exchange building, now called Beurs van Berlage, was finished in 1903, for example.

At the movement's core was the innovative use of cheap materials such as brick, wood and roof tiles. It valued the idea of integrating art disciplines through sculpture and intricate (and often curvaceous brick) details, as well as considered interiors.

The growing population and the housing shortage caused by destruction during the First World War also saw socialist, Catholic and Protestant housing corporations commission architects to build entire neighbourhoods such as Plan South and Plan West. Democratic and attractive, these were statements from the architects about beauty and art being accessible to all.

**(Pictures 01 to 03)** Olympic Stadium, Jan Wils, 1928
*2 Olympisch Stadion, 1076 DE*
**(04 to 05)** De Dageraad, Michel de Klerk and Piet Kramer, 1919 to 1922
*PL Takstraat, 1073 KK*
**(06 to 07)** Beurs Van Berlage, HP Berlage, 1903
*243 Damrak, 1012 ZJ*
**(08 to 10)** Jeruzalemkerk, Ferdinand Jantzen, 1929
*14 Jan Maijenstraat, 1056 SG*
**(11 to 13)** Vrijheidslaan, Michel de Klerk, 1921 to 1923
*Vrijheidslaan, 1078 PJ*

02    03

06

04

05    07

08

09

10

11

12

13

**1**

Museum Ons' Lieve Heer
op Solder, Centrum
*Furtive votives*

Religion in the Netherlands was
not openly tolerated in the 17th
century so discreet services had
to be held in homes. Many attics
concealed places of worship but
few have been preserved. Ons'
Lieve Heer op Solder (Our Lord in
the Attic) was built by a Catholic
merchant in 1663, spans four
buildings and is cut into the top
three storeys of canal houses.

Historians have tried to return
the church to its original design,
including the mauve of the walls
and balconies, discovered after
stripping back layers of paint.
While the audio tour, mandatory
booties and reimagined living
quarters may seem gimmicky, the
paradoxical relationship between
the church's concealment and
opulence is striking.
*38 Oudezijds Voorburgwal,*
*1012 GE*
*+31 (0)20 624 6604*
*opsolder.nl*

**2**

Architectuurcentrum Amsterdam,
Eastern Docklands
*Building on the past*

The curving Architectuurcentrum
Amsterdam (Arcam) building
was designed by Renzo Piano
and constructed as a pavilion for
the Nemo Science Museum (*see
page 116*) in 1997. When the site
was assigned to exhibitions on
architecture, urban-planning and
landscape design in 2003, Dutch
architect René van Zuuk was
enlisted to remodel it.

The existing floor and its
triangular shape with five columns
beneath were maintained. A wave-
like case of zinc-coated aluminium
was folded over the structure, while
a wall of glass provided views of the
docks. Two of the three storeys now
house simple exhibitions on the
city's design but catch the Crash
Course on Friday afternoons, when
staff run through nearly seven
centuries of architectural history.
*600 Prins Hendrikkade, 1011 VX*
*+31 (0)20 620 4878*
*arcam.nl/en*

*Please don't break,*
*please don't break*

(3)
Stadsarchief Amsterdam
De Bazel, Centrum
*Records rooms*

Karel de Bazel designed this
towering (by Amsterdam standards)
chequered stone building in 1926 for
the Dutch Trading Company. He
wanted his design to outlast fickle
trends rather than conform to any set
style. Sadly the building's subsequent
residents (which included a bank)
altered his vision, inserting partitions
and lowering ceilings.

In 2005 restoration architect
Maartin Fritz was enlisted to
reinstate de Bazel's intended
timelessness and create a home
for the city's archives. It opened as
Stadsarchief Amsterdam in 2007 and
holds extensive historical records on
the top four floors (the most valued
records are in the old basement
bank vaults). There is also a free
exhibition space that gives you a
good idea of the building's design.
*32 Vijzelstraat, 1017 HL.*
*+31 (0)20 251 1511*
*debazelamsterdam.nl;*
*archief.amsterdam*

**④**

Nemo Science Museum,
Eastern Docklands
*Find it*

Nemo's copper-green hull,
emerging from Oosterdok, is
one of the boldest designs on the
cityscape. Italian architect Renzo
Piano called Amsterdam "a one-
dimensional city" and this fuelled
his vision to create an elevated
piazza and observation terrace
on the building's roof.

Piano's main challenge was
using the IJtunnel as Nemo's
foundation. The tunnel inspired
his curved design: as it descends
below the river the museum
mirrors it, rising 22 metres above
the water. Since its completion
in 1997, Piano's design has
housed the Netherlands' leading
children's science and technology
museum. Its interior focuses
attention on exhibits by having
minimal windows, straightforward
orientation and neutral grey walls.
*2 Oosterdok, 1011 VX*
*+31 (0)20 531 3233*
*nemosciencemuseum.nl/en*

**Collect 'em all**
The museum houses 17,000 technological artefacts

**⑤**

Museum Het Schip, Westerpark
*Vessel for knowledge*

Museum Het Schip is perhaps
the most iconic example of the
Amsterdam School style, designed
by Michel de Klerk and built
between 1917 and 1921 (Eduard
Cuypers discovered De Klerk at
the age of 14 and took him on as
a pencil sharpener).

Shaped roughly like a ship,
the building has played host to
a post office, primary school
and residential block. De Klerk
finished every detail with great
care, believing that giving people
somewhere beautiful to live would
encourage them to climb the social
and economic ladder. The building
still has about 80 social-housing
apartments but a large portion
is now open to the public as a
museum. To learn more about the
movement, its techniques and the
building, arrive for the museum's
15.00 tour in English.
*45 Oostzaanstraat, 1013 WG*
*+31 (0)20 686 8595*
*hetschip.nl*

## Contemporary
Modern artistry

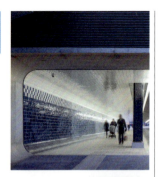

① 
Cuyperspassage, Centrum
*Underground movement*

Beneath Centraal station is the Cuyperspassage pedestrian-and-cyclist tunnel that connects the city with the ferries to the north and services 15,000 commuters a day. The 110-metre-long corridor opened in 2015 and was designed by Benthem Crouwel Architects – who also designed Rai Car Park (*see opposite*) – and graphic-design luminary Irma Boom.

Before entering, stand on the line that separates pedestrians from cyclists; the contrasting colours and lighting make the tunnel appear to split in two. The walkway is covered in 80,000 Delftware tiles, 46,000 of which depict Boom's design of the warship *Rotterdam* and the Herring Fleet. By contrast, the cycle path is unmarked asphalt and metal grates.
*Centraal station, Stationsplein, 1012 AB*

### Changing skyline

Gaining approval for development projects within the city centre is near impossible because most buildings are under Unesco World Heritage protection. As such, city-planners and developers are looking to construct commercial, residential and public buildings in the outlying suburbs. Here are a few projects to keep an eye out for.

01 **Bridge to Noord, Eastern Docklands:** The prospect of a bridge that crosses the IJ has been town-planning fodder since the early 1900s. But more concrete plans are forming for a joint pedestrian-and-cyclists bridge stretching between Java-eiland and Noord.

02 **Sluisbuurt, Zeeburgereiland:** This highly controversial plan is for a new high-rise neighbourhood on an industrial island in the IJ harbour. Residential towers will stand at about 130 metres tall, blocking the view of residents in the Noord. Construction is set to begin in 2018.

03 **Houthavens:** Construction for this climate-neutral neighbourhood on a decommissioned industrial port in the west began in 2010. A school and its gym are already open and the entire project, which will include new islands for housing blocks, is slated for completion in 2020.

### Bridges

Amsterdam has about 1,200 bridges, from 17th-century drawbridges to postmodern, minimalist crossings. Here are some favourites.

**01  Na-Druk-Geluk-Brug, Oud-Zuid:** Designed by René van Zuuk Architekten in 2013 as part of a wider regeneration in Amsterdam Zuid. Minimal detailing and stark white deliberately contrast with Jan Wils' 1928 Olympic Stadium and the industrial blocks to the south.

**02  Jan Schaeferbrug, Eastern Docklands:** Ton Venhoeven's bridge spans 200 metres and links the eastern Java-eiland with the city. Every five years, two entire sections weighing about 200 tonnes are removed by barge to allow the tall ships of Sail Amsterdam to pass.

**03  Borneo-Sporenburg, Eastern Docklands:** Two red walkways connect the Borneo and Sporenburg residential islands in the Eastern Docklands. Completed in 2000 by West 8, the higher bridge has impressive views of the marina and allows boats to pass while the lower, more accessible one mirrors it at the opposite end of the harbour.

**04  Magere Brug, Centrum:** The original Skinny Bridge dates back to 1691; the current, wider drawbridge is from 1931. It's thought to have been commissioned by two sisters who lived on opposite sides of the canal but no one knows whether "skinny" refers to their surname, physique or penny-pinching budget.

③
Rai Car Park, Zuidas
*Ramped-up genius*

Another noteworthy project from Benthem Crouwel Architects is the Rai Amsterdam Exhibition and Convention Centre carpark. The design of these two helix-shaped ramps draws comparison with the brutalist Marnixstraat Europarking complex but the co-founder, Mels Crouwel, says it came from the iconic principle of spiralling ramps. "We aimed to make it more fine and elegant," he says.

One downside if you're on foot: with a busy motorway beside it and only a narrow footpath, you may struggle to find yourself a good viewpoint.
*Europaboulevard, 1078 RV*

②
Eye Filmmuseum, Noord
*Moving imagery*

This landmark on the IJ riverfront was designed by Viennese studio Delugan Meissl, a catalyst for the regeneration of the neglected Noord. Completed in 2012 it's almost sculptural, with a dynamic shape that looks different from every angle.

The architects began with the notion that film and architecture share fundamentals such as the interplay of movement, light and space. The exterior flows into an open and bright interior with the foyer at its heart; whichever part of the building you visit, you always return to this central space.
*1 IJpromenade, 1031 KT*
*+31 (0)20 589 1400*
*eyefilm.nl*

① Gable stones, Jordaan
*Addressing an issue*

Houses weren't numbered in Amsterdam until the late 19th century so *gevelstenen* (gable stones) were put above doorways to differentiate properties. Peaking in popularity in the 16th century, they were normally decorated with symbols of the inhabitant's profession or family sign, or occasionally an image from folklore.

The city has about 850 such stone artworks including some newer examples, mostly in Jordaan. Look out for the two men and a dog on Karthuizersstraat, which is based on the fable of Amsterdam's first settlers; the writing hand on Egelantierstraat shows what was once home to a schoolmaster.

### Take it to the grave

A short cycle along the Amstel takes you to Begraafplaats Zorgvlied, a cemetery with a monolithic pavilion shaped like a tombstone and a newly built 16-metre-high crematorium with a tent-like superstructure ending in a glass-covered opening.

② De Gooyer windmill, Eastern Docklands
*Grind house*

Windmills are synonymous with the Netherlands and this octagonal former corn mill, called De Gooyer, was built in the 18th century. Its wooden frame moved between different locations until settling in its current spot in 1814.

Although the interior is closed to the public, you can still get up close thanks to the pub next door. Microbrewery Brouwerij 't IJ was founded by musician Kaspar Peterson in 1985 in the former bathhouse next to the mill. Stop by for a glass of organic beer and sit on the terrace to enjoy the view of De Gooyer.
*5 Funenkade, 1018 AL.*

## Police branding
*Eye-catching by law*

Rolled out more than two decades ago, the branding of the Dutch emergency services is iconic. The orange, blue and white 45-degree stripes started out on police cars and bikes but more recently the fire, ambulance and rescue services have adopted them.

"Our design hasn't aged despite changes in car models and technology," says Liza Enebeis, creative director at Studio Dumbar, the agency behind the look. "Our stripes can even be found on speed cameras and drones." They're so popular that a special task force has been set up to prevent members of the public illegally sticking stripes onto their own cars.

## Amsterdamse Krulletter
*Font of originality*

The curling, gregarious swirls of the traditional Amsterdamse Krulletter were fathered by Jan Willem Joseph Visser. It first started to appear in the 1940s on the windows of the city's *bruine* cafés and was funded by Heineken as a form of advertising. Visser was inspired by the late cancellaresca style, which calligraphers practised during the Dutch Golden Age.

"The letters that Visser created bear the distinctive features of the Baroque quill," says Ramiro Espinoza, Argentinian type designer and author of De Amsterdamse Krulletter (*see page 84*). "They've resisted the test of time and have been appropriated by Amsterdam's citizens as a true expression of their culture."

Bars across the city bear Visser's signage, from the oldest tavern Café Karpershoek to the wood-panelled Café Hegeraad.

## City crest
*Cross purposes*

Contrary to the implications from gimmicky tourist trinkets, Amsterdam's city crest of xxx is not in any way related to the capital's tolerant stance towards vices. Instead the symbolism falls on the opposite end of the spectrum, representing Saint Andrew's cross.

Why the city employed the emblem of a 1st-century apostle crucified on an X-shaped cross is unknown. However, a pair of pliers sporting the three letters were recently discovered during the construction of the metro line and have been dated to 1350, suggesting that xxx is one of the oldest known examples of city branding.

It's not quite the highest I've been in Amsterdam but it's close

# Sport and fitness
## —— Active city

The people of Amsterdam aren't averse to exercise – how could they be in a city that's as renowned for its bicycle culture as it is for its canals? These waterways play a key part in the outdoor culture, whether it's cycling along them or simply enjoying the passing scenery from a boat as you float peacefully down them. During the colder months, when the water sometimes freezes, you're likely to spot the locals lacing up their skates and zipping across the ice (if the weather fails to co-operate you can still participate at a range of artificial rinks).

If you prefer your exercise to be a little more traditional there are also gyms (some more punishing than others), pools and tennis courts where you can get your heart rate up, or failing that check out our recommendations for a scenic run or two. And when you're done, refresh and revive at our selection of grooming hotspots and spa destinations. You'll have earned it.

**Warmer months**
Hot in the city

Route finder
——
Don't want to drive? Mokum can provide a skipper

**①**
Boat hire, citywide
*Drift away*

During the warmer months, rent a boat, pack a picnic and float towards the harbour or Amstel River. No licence is required for rentals, just a sober captain over 18 who can handle the intersections.

Mokum Boats rental locations include Centrum, Amstel and Oost. For a snack, dock along the quays at Café Hesp, Hannekes Boom or Waterkant. Or for a swim, head south for the widened section of the Amstel in front of the tHuis aan de Amstel café.
*Mokum Boats: Centrum, 351 Nassaukade, 1053 LZ; Amstel, 1 Schollenbrugstraat, 1091 EX; Oost, 65 Mauritskade, 1092 AD mokumbootverhuur.nl*

**②**
Flevopark, Indische Buurt
*Activity centre*

Flevopark is wedged between the Indische Buurt neighbourhood and Nieuwe Diep Lake. Dutch conservationist and botanist Jac P Thijsse led the charge to develop the park to service the city's growing population; it was completed in 1931 for the Jewish community, then bought by the city in 1956 and opened to the public.

Today it's favoured by runners and in warm weather the outdoor pool opens and the lake is perfect for watersports. Barbecues are permitted in designated areas and the former watermill now houses a distillery and tasting room.
*Kramatweg, 1095 KD flevopark.nl; nwediep.nl*

## Colder months
### Just chill

Ⓘ
Ice-skating, citywide
*Blade runners*

As soon as the layer of ice on top of ditches, canals and lakes is firm, Amsterdammers get their skates on. Not every winter is cold enough nowadays, so from November to February there's an artificial rink in front of the Rijksmuseum, with skate rental and a café serving hot chocolate and glühwein.

Jaap Edenbaan in the east has a 400-metre loop open in the winter and an indoor rink all year round. During sub-zero temperatures, Amsterdamse Bosbaan in the south is the place to skate.
*Rijksmuseum: 5 Museumplein, 1071 DJ; iceamsterdam.nl*
*Jaap Edenbaan: 64 Radioweg, 1098 NJ; jaapeden.nl*

## Sporting events

**01  Dam tot Damloop:**
This annual 16km road race sees 50,000 participants run from Amsterdam through the IJtunnel and the Dutch countryside to Zaandam.
*damloop.nl*

**02  Sail Amsterdam:**
Every five years more than 600 sailing ships from across the globe drop anchor in the IJ. Festivities take place both ashore and onboard the ships.
*sail.nl*

**03  Amsterdam Marathon:**
With 16,500 runners, the annual Amsterdam Marathon tours the Eastern Docklands, Zuid, Oud-West and a pretty stretch of the Amstel River.
*tcsamsterdammarathon.nl*

**04  Amsterdam City Swim:**
More than 2,000 swimmers dive into the canals in September to swim 2,000 metres, raising funds for Amyotrophic lateral sclerosis. Even Queen Máxima has taken part.
*amsterdamcityswim.nl*

## Year-round
### Perennial favourites

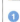

Ⓘ
High45, De Plantage
*Gonna make you sweat*

If the thought of a 45-minute fitness class doesn't seem all that daunting, think again. High45 is tough: whole-body tough, enough to make you want to tell the very nice and encouraging instructor to kindly go away.

Barbara den Bak opened this sleek studio in 2016 and bases all of her classes on the principles of high-intensity interval training. Class sizes are small, single passes are available and we can guarantee you'll feel fantastic post-workout. You might just have to wait for the waves of nausea to subside first.
*101 Weesperstraat, 1018 VN*
*+31 (0)20 890 3158*
*high45.com*

*I don't know what you're talking about, this is light as a feather*

② 
Tennisclub IJburg, IJburg
*Hi, court*

This club is a 30-minute cycle ride (by Amsterdam standards it may as well be halfway to Germany) but if you fancy a game while in town, the MVRDV-designed Tennisclub in IJburg is worth the pedal.

The ruby-red clubhouse with a café and changing rooms looks out over pristine waters and its roof doubles as a grandstand for the 10 clay courts. This public sporting complex was developed to encourage Amsterdammers out to the far-eastern neighbourhood, so visitors don't need a membership and it's open whatever the season.
*1 Zandzeggestraat, 1087 SL*
*+31 (0)20 778 1671*
*tennisverenigingijburg.nl*

**Junior service**
The club also has a court specifically for children

③ 
Zuiderbad, Oud-Zuid
*Decorative pool*

The art deco Zuiderbad, which abuts the Rijksmuseum, was designed as an indoor driving school by Jonas Ingenohl in 1897. It didn't last long and soon became a showroom, then in 1912 opened as a swimming pool. Progressive for its time, it had electric lighting, central-heating and a sand-based water-filtration system in the basement, all of which still function.

While not the best spot for serious swimmers, its mosaic tiling and brass fixtures make a dramatic setting for a few relaxing laps.
*26 Hobbemastraat, 1071 ZC*
*+31 (0)20 252 1390*
*amsterdam.nl/sport/waar-sporten/*
*zwembaden/zuiderbad*

④ 
Akasha, Oud-Zuid
*Underground club*

One level below the glass atrium of the Conservatorium Hotel is the Amsterdam outpost for Akasha. For short-term visitors, day passes and monthly membership are available. These afford access to pilates, boxing and yoga classes, the moderately sized but well-equipped gym and the underground spa with its pool, sauna and hamam.

The real treat is in the details, from the smartly designed lockers with retractable coat hangers to the Netflix-enabled screens on the treadmills.
*Conservatorium Hotel, 27 Van Baerlestraat, 1071 AN*
*+31 (0)20 570 0000*
*conservatoriumhotel.com*

## Grooming
### Looking good

**① Wild Romance, Centrum**
*Pride and grooming*

There's no shortage of good hairdressers in the Dutch capital but for the hat-trick of skilled staff, good music and strong coffee, you should consider a passionate fling with Wild Romance.

A host of seasoned freelancers operate out of the duplex studio, cutting, colouring and styling. A pretty little atrium with basins can be found up top, while a vintage-inspired barber is set up on the lower level. There's also a solid stack of the latest publications on hand including – ahem – one called Monocle. Make your booking online or in person.
*62 Spuistraat, 1012 TW*
*wildromance.net*

**② The Barber, Jordaan**
*Direct male*

Avail yourself of a trim and a haircut the classic way in this smart barber's hidden on a cross street of trendy Haarlemmerdijk. A full menu of treatments covers everything from the traditional hot-towel and straight-razor shave to The Connery, the shop's amusingly monickered head shave for the follically challenged.

As well as offering its own range of beard products, aftershaves and oils, The Barber carries a selection from the likes of Hudson Made, Mr Natty and OAK. Oh, and coffee, beer or whiskey is on the house.
*24 Binnen Oranjestraat, 1013 JA*
*+ 31 (0)20 337 3755*
*barber.nl*

**③ Spa Zuiver, Zuideramstel**
*Bare necessities*

To work out the niggles of a long flight or just a long day, head south to Spa Zuiver on the border of the Amsterdamse Bos nature reserve. There's a seemingly endless array of pools, tubs and saunas to dip in and out of, including the outdoor spa and 40-metre lap pool surrounded by forest.

Fellow bathers tend to be nude but if you're not keen on that idea, swimwear is permitted on Tuesdays and Thursdays. There are also squash and tennis courts, as well as a catering service and 31 hotel rooms.
*8 Koenenkade, 1081 KH*
*+ 31 (0)20 301 0700*
*zuiveramsterdam.nl*

### Football: Ajax

For those who concern themselves with such things, Dutch football has a mystical allure – and no team better represents this enchantment than Ajax (*see page 77*). The club's legend was sealed in the 1970s when, with Johan Cruyff, they won the European Cup three seasons in a row.

If you want to go and watch the latest incarnation of this fabled team, tickets can be bought online and collected at the ground (which can be reached by metro or bus). And if your visit doesn't coincide with a match day, you can take a guided tour instead.
*ajax.nl*

*Whoops, see you later! Just call me Johan Wooyff*

## Cycling routes
Pedal power

## Running routes
Hit the road

① 
Noord cycle tour
*Waterways and green fields*

The city centre isn't always the most relaxing place to wheel around so try the north's rural paths instead.

STARTING POINT: Centraal station, Centrum
DISTANCE: 10km

Rent your *fiets* (bicycle) from MacBike, around the back of Centraal station. Take the 902 ferry to ❶ *IJplein*, drinking in the views over the city, and once docked pedal northeast along Meeuwenlaan. Cross the first roundabout and just after the road forks take a sharp right onto pretty Nieuwendammerdijk (*see page 109*), a quaint street with charming old houses.

Take a break in ❷ *Café 't Sluisje*, a historic *bruin* café in a building that's nearly 500 years old and has a large waterside terrace that's perfect for lunch. Continue straight along the same road, passing fields and waterways as you go, until it ends at a park.

Turn right over the white bridge, immediately left and then keep right on Schellingwouderdijk. After you've passed some football pitches, turn right down Noorder IJdijk and dismount when you reach the start of the ❸ *Oranjesluizen*. To cross this series of working locks you'll have to go by foot.

Once you're back on your bike head down Zuider IJdijk, joining the two upper paths nearest the water. At the T-junction turn right and follow the path to a big bridge; wheel your bike up the tracks on the nearside stairway. Head west along Zuiderzeeweg until the junction, where you turn right onto Zeeburgerdijk. Continue for 1.5km until you see the De Gooyer windmill (*see page 120*) over the water to your right. Once you reach it, it would be impolite not to reward yourself with a beer at adjacent brewery ❹ *Brouwerij 't IJ*.

① 
Vondelpark
*Park run*

DISTANCE: 4.3km
GRADIENT: Flat
DIFFICULTY: Easy
HIGHLIGHT: The stretch along the southern pond
BEST TIME: Take your pick
NEAREST STATION: Rijksmuseum

Start at the main entrance of the park on *Stadhouderskade* and head west under the bridge designed by Piet Kramer in 1947. Next you'll enter the main park; take the first right to follow the road that loops around the pond. Look out for the neo-gothic *Vondelkerk* on the right, designed by Pierre Cuypers, the man behind the Rijksmuseum (*see page 91*). At the fork in the path, leave the main road and head right on the narrow path that meanders along the edge of the park, passing Roman church-turned-music-venue *Orgelpark*.

As you rejoin the main road, take a sharp right and carry on for about 700 metres. At the end follow the curve to your left and once you've crossed the water (marked by knee-high walls) take a right to run along the narrow path. Rejoin the main road and after about 300 metres take the lakeside path again.

At the next fork, keep left and then head back onto the main road. Veer right, passing "Figure Découpée (L'Oiseau)" in the clearing on your left. This sculpture was designed by Picasso and presented to the city in 1965. Loop right around the pond and on the left look for a blue bridge to the *Blauwe Theehuis* (Blue Teahouse), a modernist institution built in the 1930s. Finish here with a drink or loop around the building and continue on to pass the statue of Dutch poet Joost van den Vondel, after whom the park was named. You'll wind up back at the starting point.

②
Outer canal ring
*Round trip*

DISTANCE: 10km
GRADIENT: Flat
DIFFICULTY: Moderate
HIGHLIGHT: The changing architecture
BEST TIME: Early morning to beat the traffic
NEAREST STATION: Rijksmuseum

Start anywhere on the outer canal ring, depending on where you're staying; we'll start across from the *Rijksmuseum*, going anti-clockwise around Centrum. Avoid the red bike path and stick to the footpath, which sporadically becomes a carpark over the next kilometre. Cross at Weteringlaan and head along the canal past the old *Heineken Brewery*. Cross Westeinde, with De Nederlandsche Bank on your left.

The road inclines to cross the Amstel. Bear right at the Wibautstraat intersection, following the pedestrian crossings. At the statue of *Dr F M Wibaut* run east along the canal to the Olifantsbrug. Cross it, head down the passage through the building ahead, then cross Sarphatistraat and take the wooden bridge to run past the new blocks on Entrepotdok. Follow the road almost to the end, veer right down another passage, then left over the green drawbridge.

Turn right towards Arcam (*see page 114*), then left along Prins Hendrikkade. Pass by *Grand Hotel Amrâth* (*see page 24*) then as you pass Hotel NH Collection, veer right to cross the canal. At the next canal turn left then right along Haarlemmerstraat, which turns into Haarlemmerdijk retail strip. Cross the square, approach the concrete Haarlemmerpoort arcade and turn left on Korte Marnixstraat. This final leg is inside the canal ring, an uninterrupted stretch of footpath. At the Apple store head right over the canal and then left to finish by the Rijksmuseum.

③
Westerpark
*Canal tour*

DISTANCE: 5km
GRADIENT: Flat
DIFFICULTY: Moderate
HIGHLIGHT: Scenic views of canals (and a windmill)
BEST TIME: Mornings if you're a dog-lover
NEAREST STATION: Haarlemmerplein

It's easy to clock some kilometres in Westerpark. The manicured garden dotted with sculptures joins the old gasworks, now restaurants and bars, and tracks extend north and west through the less-maintained greenery.

Start at the Westerpark entrance (at the junction of *Houtmankade* and *Westerpark*), following the main footpath northwest; at the tennis courts follow the paved path as it veers slightly right. You'll soon be running in line with the train and when the path ends cross the thoroughfare (look out for cyclists) and continue along the footpath opposite.

The next leg is a simple loop around the western residential stretch of the parklands, along a gravel path with wild foliage on either side. At the carpark look for the path on your left and follow it down the gentle slope to the end. Continue adjacent to *Sloterdijkerweg* for about 200 metres then follow the path as it turns left to re-enter the parklands. Go left again at the next corner and run along the tree-lined footpath, bordered by the residential plots on your left and a commercial complex on your right.

As you approach the cylindrical building of the *Westergasfabriek* (Western Gasworks) you'll reach a junction. If you're feeling fit take a left towards and under the train line for a short lap around a city farm; if you're ready to wind down head straight back towards Westerpark. At the train line follow the path on which you entered the park.

# Walks
## — Best foot forward

It is no secret that the bicycle is considered king in Amsterdam but unfortunately that is to the detriment of pedestrians. Footpaths are often narrow, sometimes blocked and occasionally disappear altogether without warning. However, it's worth persevering because the compact nature of neighbourhoods is perfect for exploring food, retail and culture offerings on foot – just make sure you mind your step in the process.

NEIGHBOURHOOD 01

# Oost
## *On the up*

To experience the less-polished side of Amsterdam, head to the city's energetic east. Here you'll find the fruits of the Netherlands' prolific colonial exploits, particularly in the names of the streets. Once considered a part of town best avoided, today things are on the rise as students and artists arrive in search of cheaper rent and the neighbourhood becomes more diverse.

The walk begins in an area known as Oud-Oost (Old East), which is not as old as its name might suggest: it only dates back to the late 19th century and was built to give labourers more affordable housing – the Dubbeltjespanden is a particularly charming example. The area's green lung is Oosterpark, packed with interesting sculptures and inviting reading spots, and on its outskirts are several notable historical sights, including the country's biggest wooden windmill. The second half of the walk takes in the century-old Indische Buurt, named after the Dutch East Indies (present-day Indonesia). Its beating heart is Javastraat, a vibrant mix of ethnic food shops, boutiques, trendy bars and great restaurants.

Often compared to New York's Brooklyn, Oost is where the tidy picture-perfect canals of central Amsterdam give way to the grittier hustle and bustle of a truly diverse neighbourhood.

Lively spirit
*Oost walk*

Start off with a coffee and a bite to eat at ❶ *Bar Bukowski* then walk round the left-hand side of Oosterpark to find the nearest entrance. When it opened in 1891, Oosterpark was the first major public green space in the city (Vondelpark is older but was initially private). These days it's home to dozens of works of art such as ❷ *De Schreeuw*, a tribute to film-maker Theo van Gogh who was murdered in 2004 after he made a controversial film about women in Islam. The stainless-steel work is between the park's two southeastern entrances.

Leave the park heading north, keeping the Generator Hostel on your left, and join Mauritskade. Just before you hit the main road, check out ❸ *VanMoof*, an award-winning specialist bike shop that also offers free worldwide shipping. From there turn left and then immediately left again into quaint ❹ *Dubbeltjespanden* (literally, "dime buildings", named after the original weekly rental cost). This was one of the first examples of social housing in the Netherlands when construction began in 1870. The brick shelves with white silhouettes of objects tell the stories of the street's residents over the decades.

Before leaving make sure you look across the water: that feast of brick and glass is a former medicine-storage building. It was reimagined by US architect Steven Holl and is now part of a housing association.

Walk east towards the imposing Tropenmuseum (*see page 139*), which is worth a visit if you have a spare hour or two. Otherwise cross the bridge in front of it and admire the grand ❺ *Muiderpoort* archway, the only remaining gate from Amsterdam's old fortifications. It was built in the Louis XVI style in the 18th century and Napoleon rode through it in 1811 after conquering the city.

Return to the Singelgracht and walk along Alexanderkade until you reach the delightful De Gooyer windmill. The tallest in the country, it is now a private home but you

can enjoy a good view of the exterior along with a beer and some *bitterballen* (deep-fried snacks) at the neighbouring brewery, ❻ *Brouwerij 't IJ (see page 120)*.

Cross the bridge and rejoin Mauritskade before diving into one of Oost's gems: the raucous ❼ *Dappermarkt*. With stalls selling everything from Arabic rugs to fish, this is where the neighbourhood meets, mingles and shops. Take your time and amble down to Eerste van Swindenstraat and then turn left. Continue walking until you see ❽ *Roopram Roti* just before the end of the road. This place won't win any awards for decor but, as the queues suggest, it's second-to-none for Surinamese food. Try the lamb or *pom* (chicken) roti for a cheap and cheerful lunch.

Double back on yourself and continue straight ahead under the train bridge. This is the beginning of Javastraat, the perfect place to find one-off clothes and hard-to-find spices. There's an afternoon's worth of exploring to be done here but don't miss ❾ *The Other Guys* for edgy local and international fashion brands.

At the end of the street grab a burger or some freshly grilled fish at the unmissable ❿ *Het Badhuis*, a well-preserved former bathhouse that was still in use well into the second half of the 20th century.

To continue your evening, head north up Molukkenstraat to ⓫ *Bar Joost* to enjoy some more Dutch beer. Or follow Borneostraat and catch a film at ⓬ *Studio K*, a quirky student-run association that also hosts club nights and cultural events.

## Getting there

Trams 3 and 7 cross the entire city and stop at Beukenweg station next to Bar Bukowski. Metro lines 51, 53 and 54 start at Centraal station and stop at Wibautstraat, five minutes from the starting point. It is also a 10-minute cycle from the centre.

## Address book

**01  Bar Bukowski**
10 Oosterpark, 1092 AE
+31 (0)20 370 1685
*barbukowski.nl*

**02  De Schreeuw**
Oosterpark, 1092 AS

**03  VanMoof**
55 Mauritskade, 1092 AD
+31 (0)20 330 7401
*vanmoof.com*

**04  Dubbeltjespanden**
29-54 Mauritskade,
1092 AA
*dubbeltjespanden.nl*

**05  Muiderpoort**
500 Sarphatistraat,
1018 AV

**06  Brouwerij 't IJ**
7 Funenkade, 1018 AZ
+31 (0)20 528 6237
*brouwerijhetij.nl*

**07  Dappermarkt**
Dapperstraat, 1093 BS
+31 (0)20 694 7495
*dappermarkt.nl*

**08  Roopram Roti**
4 Eerste van
Swindenstraat, 1093 GC
+31 (0)20 693 2902
*roopramroti.nl*

**09  The Other Guys**
51 Javastraat, 1094 HA
+31 (0)20 233 7825

**10  Het Badhuis**
21 Javaplein, 1095 CJ
+31 (0)20 665 1226
*badhuis-javaplein.nl*

**11  Bar Joost**
33 Molukkenstraat,
1095 AT
+31 (0)62 903 6092
*joost-amsterdam.nl*

**12  Studio K**
62 Timorplein, 1094 CC
+31 (0)20 692 0422
*studio-k.nu*

NEIGHBOURHOOD 02
# Oud-West
*Creatively inclined*

Centuries ago this neighbourhood was little more than farmland, home to a smattering of country residences belonging to the rich and the location for some of Amsterdam's less-salubrious establishments, such as tanneries and a plague house. It wasn't until the late 19th century that construction began in earnest to make room for working-class families, meaning that, like Oud-Oost, Oud-West is not as old as you might think.

The area has been gentrified over the past decade, introducing new shops, cafés, bars and restaurants beloved by the city's creative residents. While it lacks museums and other traditional tourist attractions there are plenty of examples of clever rejuvenation, from a former tram depot to an old pathology laboratory, as well as an array of Amsterdam School buildings. Home to nearly 180 different nationalities, the neighbourhood's diversity is evident in its proximity to Westermoskee – the largest mosque in the Netherlands – and the bustling Ten Kate Market. At the same time, the area continues to feel traditionally Dutch and many of the streets are named after notable national poets, including Johannes Kinker (look out for the plaques).

This walk will lead you through this compact and casual area and invite you to follow in the footsteps of its residents.

Architecture and art
*Oud-West walk*

Start in Kwakersplein, a square that was once a lake surrounded by windmills. Keep an eye out for ❶ *De Ratelaar*, a bronze statue that honours the city's rubbish-collectors. The sound of their rattles calling for people to bring their rubbish out was once a key part of Amsterdam's soundscape. Behind the sculpture is ❷ *Berry*, where you can grab a coffee and a muffin.

Cross the canal and turn left onto the tiny Tollensstraat to reach the ❸ *De Hallen* complex. A former tram depot, it now houses a cinema, indoor food market, hairdresser, dance studio and several independent shops selling everything from olive oil and ceramics to jeans and photography. Enter the small building on your left first and walk through the larger building opposite. Exit onto the truly local ❹ *Ten Kate Market*, a great place for people-watching.

Head west along Bellamystraat, a historical street with a village

feel. The ❺ *Olympiagebouw* started out as a stable yard for a Dutch delivery company, then from the 1920s to the 1960s was a neighbourhood cinema known as the "flea pit". It later became a mosque and Turkish cultural centre and today it's a dance school.

Walk to Tweede Kostverlorenkade and pause to take in the massive ❻ *Westermoskee* across the water. The biggest mosque in the Netherlands, it was designed by French architects Marc and Nada Breitman, who

Bellamystraat　　Kwakersstraat

Kinkerbrug

Eerste
Helmersstraat

used red brick and other features inspired by Amsterdam School and architect HP Berlage to make it blend in with its surroundings. It was – and still is – controversial and took 20 years to complete.

Walk left along the canal and cross the next bridge towards Het Sieraad. An excellent example of Amsterdam School architecture with its curving brick façade and embellishments, this iconic building started life in the 1920s as a trade school. The adjoining **7** *Lokaal Edel* is the perfect place to enjoy a cold beer and some lunch on the large canal-side terrace.

Appetite sated, cross back over the same bridge and take the second right off Kinkerstraat and onto Jan Pieter Heijestraat, a hidden gem of a shopping street. **8** *Dépôt by Johnny at the Spot* has wonderfully unusual homeware and clothes, for example. Once you've finished pottering around the area, cross over Jacob van Lennepkanaal and immediately turn left. At the end of Jacob van Lennepkade you'll find a wall with several small **9** *Hildo Krop*

*sculptures*. Krop was arguably one of the most important Amsterdam School artists.

Behind the wall is a building that used to be the pathology and anatomy laboratory for nearby Wilhelmina Hospital. It has now been transformed into a creative hub with shared offices, a great café and an arthouse cinema. It's known as **10** *Lab 111*.

Walking south, turn onto Eerste Helmersstraat to find the grand entrance to the former hospital, a sprawling complex built on the site of the city's 17th-century plague house. Opened in 1893, the hospital was in action for 90 years before being converted into flats, artists' residences, a hostel and a café known as the **11** *WG-square*. Go through the archway and explore the site before returning to Eerste Constantijn Huygensstraat.

Turn left and continue walking for a few minutes until you get to **12** *Happyhappyjoyjoy*. With a large menu of Asian drinks and street food, this is the perfect place to end the walk and start your evening.

### Getting there

Trams 3 and 12 stop at Kinkerstraat while trams 7 and 17 (from Centraal station) stop at Bilderdijk/ Kinkerstraat, both of which are a one-minute walk from the starting point. It is also a 10-minute cycle from the centre.

### Address book

**01 De Ratelaar**
Kwakersplein, 1053 VH

**02 Berry**
27 Bilderdijkkade, 1053 VH
+31 (0)20 370 7300
*berryamsterdam.nl*

**03 De Hallen**
47 Hannie Dankbaarpassage, 1053 RT
+31 (0)20 705 8164
*dehallen-amsterdam.nl*

**04 Ten Kate Market**
97-99 Ten Katestraat, 1053 CC
*tenkatemarkt.nl*

**05 Olympiagebouw**
49 Bellamystraat, 1053 BG

**06 Westermoskee**
101 Piri Reïsplein, 1057 KH
*westermoskee.nl*

**07 Lokaal Edel**
1 Postjesweg, 1057 DT
+31 (0)20 799 5000
*edelamsterdam.nl*

**08 Dépôt by Johnny at the Spot**
90-94 Jan Pieter Heijestraat, 1053 GS
+31 (0)20 489 3868

**09 Hildo Krop sculptures**
305 Nicolaas Beetsstraat, 1054 PD

**10 Lab 111**
111 Arie Biemondstraat, 1054 PD
+31 (0)20 616 9994
*lab111.nl*

**11 WG-square**
9 Helmersplantsoen, 1054 RZ

**12 Happyhappyjoyjoy**
158HS Bilderdijkstraat, 1083 LC
+31 (0)20 344 6433
*happyhappyjoyjoy.asia*

NEIGHBOURHOOD 03

# Jordaan
## *Hot property*

Jordaan is arguably one of the most well-known neighbourhoods not only in Amsterdam but in the Netherlands. Its decades-long path to gentrification has seen galleries, top restaurants and high-end independent retail transform the area.

The neighbourhood was initially built when the city centre and its network of canals was doubled in the early 17th century. The area was developed for both industry and the working classes, who would service those living in the prestigious canal ring nearby. Warehouses for breweries, paper mills and small-scale factories were built along the wider canals to allow access for cargo liners. While wandering, cast your eyes up to the gable stones hinting at what the buildings once housed.

Workers' homes were built narrow as property taxes were calculated on the width of the façades; by the 19th century the overcrowded area had become a slum. However, some wealthier families funded construction of residential blocks for the poor. *Hofjes*, as they were known, were built around a courtyard and adhered to a set of rules enforced by a regent. Rooms were diminutive but many have now been renovated to align with modern standards. Today, close-knit residents and an increasingly international community populate the quiet cobbled streets. It's easy to see why Jordaan is a desirable place to dwell.

History lesson
*Jordaan walk*

Begin with a simple breakfast and a coffee at **1** *Kessens*. Co-owner Casper Holtkamp's family runs the city's much-loved Patisserie Holtkamp and the pastries also feature on Kessens' menu. Exit and head east to cross the canal and take the first left passing Westerkerk to reach the **2** *Anne Frank House*. Between 09.00 and 15.30 you can only enter if you've bought tickets in advance, so do book ahead. The

museum tells the poignant story of Anne Frank and the Netherlands during the Holocaust.

Exit the museum and walk north to Leliegracht, then cross the canal and turn right. Cross yet another bridge and head west, then take the first right and stop at **3** *Back Beat Records* to pick up some soul, funk or jazz on vinyl. Walk north on Eerste Tuindwarsstraat for another couple of blocks to reach **4** *Nils Kalf Schoenmaker* on the corner. Cobbler Nils Kalf has been making and repairing shoes for three decades.

Head north on Eerste Anjeliersdwarsstraat and continue onto Tweede Boomdwarsstraat, then turn left on Karthuizersstraat. At the entrance to houses 89 to 171 follow the stone tiles through to the inner courtyard of **5** *Karthuizer Hofje*. This particular *hofje* (almshouse) opened in 1650 to house widows and their children and was the largest of its kind in the city. Exit back past the original clotheslines and head right to the end of the street, then right again and left onto the bustling strip of Westerstraat.

On the opposite side of the street is nostalgia-packed toyshop ⑥ *Mechanisch Speelgoed*. After exploring the floor-to-ceiling collection of toys, continue along Westerstraat until you pick up the scent of freshly baked apple pie. The petite ⑦ *Winkel 43* kitchen works tirelessly to keep up with demand and the lunch menu comes recommended if you're after something savoury.

Across the street is the protestant ⑧ *Noorderkerk*, dating from the 16th century. The church was painstakingly restored between 1989 and 2005 and hosts a classical concert every Saturday at 14.00 from September to June. Head east across the square and cross the canal twice, first at Lekkeresluis then at Papiermolensluis, and take note of the two dried fish above the entrance of ⑨ *162 Brouwersgracht*. From 1821 to 1971 the fish merchant Smit & Zoon operated from this warehouse.

Turn 180 degrees to snap a postcard-ready picture of the canal houses then walk north on Korte Prinsengracht and cross the bridge on your left before heading west on Haarlemmerdijk. An entire afternoon can be whiled away on this retail strip. We recommend taking a look around menswear and homeware shop ⑩ *Six and Sons* at number 31 and cookbook specialist ⑪ *De Kookboekhandel* at number 133.

After your retail fix, head back south via Binnen Dommersstraat, crossing the drawbridge to walk east along Brouwersgracht, named after the breweries that once populated the warehouses along this canal. With beer in mind, stop in for a lager or two at the homely corner spot ⑫ *Café Thijssen*, named after Jordaan resident and writer Theo Thijssen.

When hunger strikes, exit the bar and turn right, stopping outside ⑬ *55 Lindengracht* to look up at the humorous gable stone of a topsy-turvy world. Unlike the other centuries-old stones in the area, this one is from 1972 and nods to the fact that the street was a canal until 1895. Finish your walk with an Italian meal just a few doors down at ⑭ *Toscanini*.

### Getting there

Trams 13, 14 and 17 servicing Oud-West, the centre and Eastern Docklands all stop at Westermarkt Station, which is a two-minute walk from the starting point. Alternatively, if you're on two wheels, Jordaan is a 10 to 15-minute pedal from most central locations.

## Address book

**01 Kessens**
24 Rozengracht, 1016 NC
+31 (0)20 221 7431
*kessensamsterdam.nl*

**02 Anne Frank House**
263-267 Prinsengracht, 1016 GV
+31 (0)20 556 7105
*annefrank.org*

**03 Back Beat Records**
19 Egelantiersstraat, 1015 PV
+31 (0)20 627 1657
*backbeat.nl*

**04 Nils Kalf Schoenmaker**
2A Eerste Tuindwarsstraat, 1015 RV
+31 (0)20 623 4962
*nilskalfschoenmaker.nl*

**05 Karthuizer Hofje**
157 Karthuizersstraat, 1015 LP

**06 Mechanisch Speelgoed**
67 HS Westerstraat, 1015 LW
+31 (0)20 638 1680
*mechanisch-speelgoed.nl*

**07 Winkel 43**
43 Noordermarkt, 1015 NA
+31 (0)20 623 0223
*winkel43.nl*

**08 Noorderkerk**
44-48 Noordermarkt, 1015 NA
+31 (0)62 420 5631
*noorderkerk.nl*

**09 162 Brouwersgracht**
1013 HA

**10 Six and Sons**
31 Haarlemmerdijk, 1013 KA
+31 (0)20 233 0092
*sixandsons.com*

**11 De Kookboekhandel**
133 Haarlemmerdijk, 1013 KG
+31 (0)20 622 4768
*kookboekhandel.com*

**12 Café Thijssen**
107 Brouwersgracht, 1015 GD
+31 (0)20 623 8994
*cafethijssen.nl*

**13 55 Lindengracht** 1015 KC

**14 Toscanini**
75 Lindengracht, 1015 KD
+31 (0)20 623 2813
*restauranttoscanini.nl*

NEIGHBOURHOOD 04
# Bos en Lommer and De Baarsjes
*Back to school*

Strolling on foot from Rembrandtpark through De Baarsjes and up to Erasmuspark in Bos en Lommer is a good way to take in Amsterdam School style (*see page 112*). As the city struggled to deal with a housing shortage after the First World War, swathes of farmland were redeveloped and architects were commissioned by housing corporations to design entire neighbourhoods. After designing Plan Zuid, modernist Dutch architect HP Berlage drafted Plan West, which lies within this neighbourhood.

A team of 16 Amsterdam School architects, including Johan van der Mey and Piet Kramer, helped design the grids of distinct brick apartment blocks. Two architects and the head of public works supervised each design to maintain cohesion. About 6,000 homes were built over a two-year period and Berlage himself designed Mercatorplein, the nucleus of community life.

These structures have since survived the Second World War and the demolition-happy councils of the late 20th century. Today the adjoining neighbourhoods continue to expand and the young, multicultural demographic is growing. It's true that Mercatorplein and Jan Evertsenstraat can still feel a little rough around the edges but the independent retailers and restaurants have started moving in.

School trip
*Bos en Lommer and
De Baarsjes walk*

Begin with a hearty breakfast at
**1** *Café DS*. Tucked away at the back of an industrial complex, this retro dining room (think palms, chequered floors and the odd pink wall) is part of entertainment venue De School (*see page 97*).

After some eggs and a quick peek around the complex, head out past the Reade medical centre, cross over the bridge and pass the Ramada Apollo hotel to enter **2** *Rembrandtpark*. Named after the prolific Dutch painter Rembrandt Harmenszoon van Rijn, the park was opened in 1958 and has a petting zoo, outdoor gym and prime picnicking spots.

Follow the pedestrian path east to cross the lake or meander a little further south before exiting on Willem Schoutenstraat. Head east past the rows of Amsterdam School housing blocks and continue as the road gives way to a footpath. Turn left on Vasco Da Gamastraat, left again at the

end of the street then hook a right onto Vespuccistraat past the newer residential builds.

When you emerge onto the high street of Jan Evertsenstraat, traverse the pedestrian crossing to your right and enter the verdant retailer **3** *De Balkonie*. As the name suggests, this shop stocks all the mod cons you could ever wish for when decorating your balcony. Pick up some flower bulbs or a luggage-friendly pot then walk west and stop for a massage at **4** *Het Massagehuys*.

### Getting there

Tram 13 and bus routes 302
and 752, all from Centraal
station, stop just outside De
School. Alternatively, tram
7 from the east stops just
outside White Label Coffee
and is a five-minute walk
from the starting point.

Next stop is **5** *White Label Coffee*.
The brand has been roasting some
of the city's best beans since 2013;
we recommend one of the heady
filter coffees. Continue west, then
turn right at Aladdin's to walk
beneath the clock tower and turn
right again.

The street opens out onto a
square with the boxy red-brick
**6** *Jeruzalemkerk* on the northern
edge. Completed by Ferdinand
Jantzen in 1929, the church was
designed to fit in with the
surrounding Amsterdam School
architecture. Weather permitting, pull
up a chair in the square and enjoy a
*borrel* (drink) at **7** *Café Cook*.

To continue your Amsterdam
School appreciation tour, leave
Café Cook and walk east on Jan
Maijenstraat then turn left onto
**8** *Vespuccistraat*. When the leaves
on the ginkgo biloba trees change
colour in autumn, this is one of the
most picturesque streets of the Plan
West development. Completed by
Jordanus Roodenburgh in 1926,
the street was designed as a pretty
pathway between Mercatorplein
and Erasmuspark.

With this in mind, bear north
towards the park but before you
enter take a right on Jan van
Galenstraat to reach **9** *Vier
Windstrekenbrug*. Each corner
of the bridge features a sculpture
by Dutch artist Hildo Krop,
representing the Earth's four
cardinal points: there's an Inuit and
seals for the north; a warrior and
lions for the south; a Chinese man
and trading ships for the east; and a
man wearing a suit and holding a
telephone for the west.

Once you've seen all four
posts, take the stairs guarded by
sculptor Jan Trapman's polar bear
and tiger down to **10** *Erasmuspark*.
This park opened in 1939 and was
named after the Dutch renaissance
theologian Desiderius Erasmus.
The flower garden on the opposite
side of the canal bursts with colour
during spring.

After a lap around the park
return to the northern corner and
cross the bridge to walk through
Wachterliedplantsoen. Pass the
playground and basketball court
then turn right on Reinaert de
Vosstraat and left on Merlijnstraat,
continuing until you reach the stark
white tiles of **11** *Podium Mozaïek*.
This former church now acts as a
cultural hub for the west. After
catching a live show or simply
admiring how the light streams into
the building through the patterned
tiles, walk west along Bos en
Lommerweg.

Just after Hoofdweg, pass
beneath the brick building and
cut diagonally across the grass
to finish with a wood-fired pizza
and a craft beer at **12** *Wilde Westen*.

NEIGHBOURHOOD 05
# De Pijp
## *Bohemian energy*

The name "The Pipe" most likely refers to a narrow stretch of water that once cut through this neighbourhood. At the end of the 19th century the ditch was drained and replaced with the expansive market on Albert Cuypstraat. The market's diversity has permeated De Pijp's character and the high concentration of international cuisine, from Moroccan to Surinamese, is testament to the 140-plus nationalities that live and work here. Today the market itself may be a tourist trap but the wider neighbourhood has preserved its original bohemian energy.

Artists, students and writers moved in at the beginning of the 20th century, transforming the area into the city's Latin Quarter. Oude Pijp is still home to artists, who mark their studios with the sign: "Made in De Pijp". The neighbourhood's proximity to the northern canal district and its affordable (though rising) rent also appeal to creative entrepreneurs and independent-shop owners on Gerard Doustraat.

Nieuwe Pijp is more tranquil and residential. An early 20th-century Haussmann-style plan was never realised and instead made way for a social-democratic plan prioritising low-cost housing. This once-quiet area is slowly filling out with restaurants and bars and the highlight is the Dageraad, an architectural tour de force.

Market meander
*De Pijp walk*

Start with a *kopje koffie* (cup of coffee) and breakfast at **1** *Vinnies* then head north towards Ferdinand Bolstraat and cross over the Amstelkanaal, passing the petite cone-shaped bridge houses designed by Amsterdam School architect Piet Kramer. Turn right to amble along the canal (the southern border of De Pijp) until you reach Pieter Lodewijk Takstraat. Pause on the corner, looking up at the integrated sculptures of Hildo Krop perched on the Berlage Lyceum. Here begins the Dageraad, which was commissioned by the eponymous housing association and completed in 1921. The visionary social-housing estate by Michel de Klerk and Piet Kramer contains 294 flats and became a monument for the labour movement.

As you walk up Pieter Lodewijk Takstraat admire the brickwork and uniform windows. At the junction look back at one of the flagship buildings of the movement, which

now houses the **2** *Bezoekerscentrum De Dageraad.* This information centre operates under the Museum Het Schip (*see page 117*) and is dedicated to the Amsterdam School movement. Pop in to explore further or simply marvel at the decorative masonry on the façade.

Veer right along Burgemeester Tellegenstraat then turn left onto Coöperatiehof; at the end of the street, head north. Turn left at Karel du Jardinstraat, right through the Van der Helstplein and left again onto the Rustenburgerstraat. You

**Address book**

**01** **Vinnies**
45 BG Scheldestraat,
1078 GG
+31 (0)20 737 3180
*vinnieshomepage.com*

**02** **Bezoekerscentrum De
Dageraad**
128 Burgemeester
Tellegenstraat, 1073 KG
+31 (0)20 686 8595
*hetschip.nl*

**03** **CT Coffee & Coconuts**
282-284 Ceintuurbaan,
1072 LR
+31 (0)20 354 1104
*coffeeandcoconuts.com*

**04** **Sarphati Viewpoint**
Sarphatipark, 1073

**05** **Original Stroopwafels**
134 Albert Cuypstraat,
1073 BC
+31 (0)61 234 5678

**06** **Volendammer Vishandel**
Eerste van der Helstraat
60, 1072 NX
+31 20 676 0394

**07** **Bloemenhandel Sijmons**
130 Albert Cuypstraat,
1073 VZ

**08** **Charlie + Mary**
84 Gerard Doustraat,
1072 VW
+31 (0)20 662 8281
*charliemary.com*

**09** **Felice Home of Brands**
88 Gerard Doustraat,
1072 HS
+31 (0)20 774 0607
*felicehomeofbrands.com*

**10** **Fenix Books**
88 Frans Halsstraat,
1072 BW
+31 (0)20 673 9459
*fenixbooks.com*

**11** **Café Caron**
28 Frans Halsstraat,
1072 BS
*cafecaron.nl*

**12** **Wijnbar Boelen & Boelen**
50 Eerste van der
Helststraat, 1072 NV
+31 (0)20 671 2242
*wijnbar.nl*

## Getting there

The starting point is a 10-minute cycle from the canal ring. Alternatively, Scheldestraat Station is a block away and is serviced by tram 12 from the west, bus 65 from the Eastern Docklands and bus 246 that passes through Centrum.

will notice the change in architecture, indicating you are moving towards Oude Pijp.

When you hit the busy Ferdinand Bolstraat, turn right and at the Ceintuurbaan, right again. Stop for another coffee or a fresh ginger tea at ❸ *CT Coffee & Coconuts* and look up at the 1920s art deco façade of this former cinema complex. Once refuelled, head east.

When you pass Rialto cinema (arthouse enthusiasts take note) cross the street and continue, then turn right into Sarphatipark, named after Samuel Sarphati, physician and advocate for the wellbeing of the working classes. Walk northeast to the ❹ *Sarphati Viewpoint* on the bridge. Take in the views of the park designed in the English-garden style. Follow the footpath southeast to the exit then turn left and left again to stroll among the cheese and tulip stalls along Albert Cuypstraat. If you're hungry, grab a *stroopwafel* from ❺ *Original Stroopwafels* market stall or a pickled-herring sandwich at ❻ *Volendammer Vishandel*.

Take a right at the pedestrian-only Eerste van der Helststraat, passing through Gerard Douplein, then head west to wholesale flower shop ❼ *Bloemenhandel Sijmons*. Here you can buy a bouquet of wild flowers away from the Albert Cuyp crowds. Double back and enjoy an afternoon of shopping at an array of independent retailers, including concept stores ❽ *Charlie + Mary* and ❾ *Felice Home of Brands*. Next, head north along the pretty Frans Halsstraat and browse the collection of English secondhand books at ❿ *Fenix Books*.

Stroll north for three blocks to Parisian-bistro-style ⓫ *Café Caron*. Chef Alain Caron and his sons serve a range of rustic French classics, including escargots and charcuterie platters.

End the evening with a nightcap at the Netherlands' first winebar, ⓬ *Wijnbar Boelen & Boelen*. Reach it by walking east on Eerste Jacob van Campenstraat, then cutting across the Marie Heinekenplein (with the Heineken Brewery looming above) and turning right onto Eerste van der Helstraat.

# Resources
—— Inside knowledge

This is a small city with plenty to offer visitors so to help you make the most of it we've compiled a few pertinent tips. Here's a round-up of how to navigate the canals, things to do come rain or shine and the calendar of events to plan your trip around. We've also put together a classic Amsterdam playlist and some useful words to get you under the skin of Dutch culture.

## Transport
### Get around town

**01** **Train:** This is the fastest way to get into the city from Schiphol Airport, with frequent trains reaching Centraal station in about 20 minutes.
*ns.nl*

**02** **Bicycle:** Amsterdam is ideally set up for cyclists and there are plenty of rental shops to choose from. Familiarise yourself with road rules before heading out (*see page 14*).

**03** **Tram:** Other than by bicycle, this is the most convenient way to travel. The conductor's booth at the back of each tram sells one-hour, 24-hour and 48-hour travel cards that are valid on trams, buses and the metro. Those with an I Amsterdam City Card (which also gives you museum entry) travel free. The 9292 website is a good place to start planning your journey.
*9292.nl*

**04** **Bus:** The slow but extensive bus network reaches far into Amsterdam's suburbs. Night buses no longer accept cash.

**05** **Metro:** The four metro lines largely serve the suburbs but lines 51, 53 and 54 do run between east Amsterdam and Centraal station. The much-delayed Noord-Zuidlijn line is due to open in 2018.

**06** **Ferry:** Several free ferries cross the IJ river to north Amsterdam, with line 901/907 running all night. You can take your bicycle on board, of course.
*ilovenoord.com/ferry*

**07** **Taxis and cars:** Taxi ranks are plentiful and can be found throughout the city, while Uber and similar apps will show other taxi options. Parking is difficult and expensive, particularly in the centre, but if you must drive then it's more practical to use the park-and-ride schemes around the city.
*iamsterdam.com*

## Vocabulary
### Local lingo

Most Dutch people speak fluent English but just in case, here are some key words. Quick tip: "j" is like "y" in "yacht".

**01** **Hallo/hoi:** Hello/hi
**02** **Dank je wel:** Thank you
**03** **Dag/doei:** Bye
**04** **Proost:** Cheers
**05** **Jammer:** Too bad
**06** **Potverdorie:** Damn
**07** **Nog een biertje/wijn:** One more beer/wine
**08** **Mijn fiets is kapot:** My bike is broken

## Soundtrack to the city
### Five top tunes

From a track by a homegrown house heavyweight to a moving French tribute to Dutch mariners, our soundtrack to Amsterdam is as varied as the city itself.

**01** **The Beatles, 'The Ballad of John and Yoko':** They memorialised their infamous world peace "bed-in" at the Amsterdam Hilton so this is a reminder of the city's counter-cultural history.

**02** **Jacques Brel, 'Amsterdam':** A song about the seedy underside of the city's mercantile backbone and the human cost of that success. David Bowie later recorded an English version.

**03** **MC Miker G & DJ Sven, 'Holiday Rap':** A one-hit wonder from 1986 with two Dutch guys rapping over a Madonna sample. Pure and cheesy good times.

**04** **Tiesto, 'Adagio for Strings':** Both industrially modern and historically poignant, this club banger from the Dutch electronic dance-music icon hits all the right notes.

**05** **The Ex, 'Squat!':** This fired-up track from the Dutch punks captures the anger that fuelled a notable squatting scene in the 1980s.

## Best events
### What to see

**01 Keukenhof:** The world's largest flower gardens open every spring so you can admire fields full of tulips. *March, keukenhof.nl*

**02 Restaurant Week:** Look out for discounted menus across the city. *March-April, restaurantweek.nl*

**03 King's Day:** A national celebration turns Amsterdam into a sea of orange with citywide street parties. *27 April*

**04 Taste of Amsterdam:** Foodie festival in Amstelpark offering tasting dishes from some of the best chefs. *June, tasteofamsterdam.com*

**05 Holland Festival:** Biggest and oldest international arts festival in the Netherlands, with theatre, dance, music, opera, film and much more. *June, hollandfestival.nl*

**06 Open Garden Days:** A chance to peek at the private gardens and interiors of some canal houses. *June, opentuinendagen.nl*

**07 Kwaku Festival:** A multicultural event commemorating the abolition of slavery in Dutch colonies, with music, food, markets, football and dance. *July-August, kwakufestival.nl*

**08 Gay Pride:** One of the biggest and best pride celebrations in the world, with a week of exhibitions, parties and events that peaks with the Canal Parade. *July-August, pride.amsterdam*

**09 Amsterdam Heritage Days:** Historical buildings, monuments and private homes throw open their doors to the public free of charge. *September, amsterdam.nl*

**10 International Documentary Film Festival Amsterdam:** The biggest festival of its kind in the world with some 300 films. *November, idfa.nl*

## Rainy days
### Weather-proof activities

**01 Culture galore:** Amsterdam is brimming with excellent museums and galleries, from the Stedelijk to Rembrandthuis. The oft-overlooked Tropenmuseum (Museum of the Tropics), tucked away in a beautiful old building next to Oosterpark, is another wonderful option with several floors of fascinating objects, photographs, music, film and interactive displays about non-western culture. The regularly changing exhibits look at themes such as mourning, celebration and prayer. It's particularly good for children. *tropenmuseum.nl*

**02 Explore Westergasfabriek:** The former gasworks complex in west Amsterdam has numerous things to do if the weather takes a turn for the worse. Browse a food market, join a yoga class, enjoy mussels and a gin and tonic, sit for some wine-tasting, catch an indie film, play arcade games while you nibble on Japanese food, visit the brewery or watch some live jazz. The architecture of the red-brick buildings is an interesting attraction in itself. *westergasfabriek.nl*

**03 Take to the water:** Amsterdam still manages to look charming in the rain and if the weather is awful while you're visiting, a great way to sightsee and stay dry is to join a canal boat tour. Operator Rederij P Kooij is nearly a century old and remains a family business, offering informative hour-long tours of the city centre for a reasonable rate in fully covered boats. Its impressive guestbook includes famous names such as Winston Churchill, Michael Jackson and Nelson Mandela. *rederijkooij.nl*

## Sunny days
### The great outdoors

**01 Park life:** Amsterdammers love their parks and Vondelpark in the south of the city, with its wending waterways and secluded spots, remains a beautiful place to while away an afternoon. Barbecues have recently been banned but picnics are still allowed and there are several good cafés to choose from if you haven't pre-packed your food and drink. Look out for Picasso's sculpture "The Fish", tucked away in a corner of the park. *hetvondelpark.net*

**02 Cycle it out:** Offering a scenic respite from the bustle of Amsterdam, Ouderkerk aan de Amstel is about a half-hour cycle from the city centre yet it feels a world away. The quaint village dates back to the 12th century and is home to historical churches, the De Zwaan windmill and a 400-year-old Jewish cemetery, the oldest in the Netherlands. The trip takes you along the banks of the Amstel River, from which Amsterdam takes its name.

**03 Beach day:** Although the city has its fair share of great urban beaches such as Pllek (see page 31), nothing beats the real thing. When the weather warms up one of the most popular places to go is Bloemendaal aan Zee, a short train ride from the city. A range of wind and water sports are on offer here, including kitesurfing, stand-up paddle boarding and catamaran sailing. The beach has several upmarket bars and beach clubs offering everything from snacks to sophisticated lunches. When the sun goes down you can kick back with a cocktail, enjoy some relaxed dining or join in with one of the lively beach parties, outdoor cinema events or live gigs.

# About Monocle
## —— Step inside

In 2007, Monocle was launched as a monthly magazine briefing on global affairs, business, culture, design and much more. We believed there was a globally minded audience of readers who were hungry for opportunities and experiences beyond their national borders.

Today Monocle is a complete media brand with print, audio and online elements – plus to mention our expanding network of shops and cafés. Besides our London HQ we have seven international bureaux in New York, Toronto, Istanbul, Singapore, Tokyo, Zürich and Hong Kong. We continue to grow and flourish and at our core is the simple belief that there will always be a place for a print brand that is committed to telling fresh stories and sending photographers on assignments. It's also a case of knowing that our success is all down to the readers, advertisers and collaborators who have supported us along the way.

**London HQ**
——
Our editorial office is in Marylebone

**❶ International bureaux**
*Boots on the ground*

We have an HQ in London and call upon firsthand reports from our contributors in more than 35 cities around the world. We also have seven international bureaux. For this travel guide, MONOCLE reporters Mikaela Aitken, Nolan Giles and Joleen Goffin decamped to the Dutch capital to explore all that it has to offer. They also called on the assistance of writers in the city, including our correspondent Venetia Rainey, to ensure that we have covered the best in retail, food, hospitality and entertainment. The aim is to make you, the reader, feel like a local when visiting this liberal city.

**❷ Online**
*Digital delivery*

We have a dynamic website: *monocle.com*. As well as being the place to hear our radio station, Monocle 24, the site presents our films, which are beautifully shot and edited by our in-house team and provide a fresh perspective on our stories. Check out the films celebrating the cities that make up our Travel Guide Series before you explore the rest of the site.

**❸ Retail and cafés**
*Food for thought*

Via our shops in Hong Kong, Toronto, New York, Tokyo, London and Singapore we sell products that cater to our readers' tastes and are produced in collaboration with brands we believe in. We also have cafés in Tokyo and London. And if you are in the UK capital visit the Kioskafé in Paddington, which combines good coffee and great reads.

**4**

Print
*Committed to the page*

MONOCLE is published 10 times a year. We have stayed loyal to our belief in quality print with two extra seasonal publications: THE FORECAST, packed with key insights into the year ahead, and THE ESCAPIST, our summer travel-minded magazine. To sign up visit *monocle.com/subscribe*. Since 2013 we have also been publishing books, like this one, in partnership with Gestalten.

**5**

Radio
*Sound approach*

Monocle 24 is our round-the-clock radio station that was launched in 2011. It delivers global news and shows covering foreign affairs, urbanism, business, culture, food and drink, design and print media. When you find yourself in Amsterdam tune into *The Globalist*, our morning news programme that is the perfect way to start the day in Europe. We also have a playlist to accompany you day and night, regularly assisted by live band sessions that are hosted at our Midori House headquarters in London. You can listen live or download any of our shows from *monocle.com*, iTunes or SoundCloud.

**Priority service**
—
Subscribers save 10 per cent in our online shop

## Join the club

**01**
**Subscribe to Monocle**
A subscription is a simple way to make sure that you never miss an issue – and you'll enjoy many additional benefits.

**02**
**Be in the know**
Our subscribers have exclusive access to the entire Monocle archive and priority access to selected product collaborations at *monocle.com*.

**03**
**Stay in the loop**
Subscription copies are delivered to your door at no extra cost no matter where you are in the world. We also offer an auto-renewal service to ensure that you never miss an issue.

**04**
**And there's more...**
Subscribers benefit from a 10 per cent discount at all Monocle shops, including online, and receive exclusive offers and invitations to events around the world.

**Choose your package**

**Premium one year**
12 × issues
+ Porter Sub Club bag
—
**One year**
12 × issues
+ Monocle Voyage tote bag
—
**Six months**
6 × issues

# Amsterdam
## Acknowledgements ———

**Chief photographer**
Jussi Puikkonen

**Still life**
David Sykes

**Writers**
Mikaela Aitken
Carole Baijings
Sanne Bolten
Robert Bound
Melkon Charchoglyan
Yoko Choy
Sabine de Witte
Hans den Hartog Jager
Pauline den Hartog Jager
Ramiro Espinoza
Nolan Giles
Joleen Goffin
Vicky Hampton
Daphne Karnezis
Pete Kempshall
Marie-Anne Leuty
Brian Maston
Mirik Milan
Alice Pfeiffer
Dan Poole
Venetia Rainey
Chiara Rimella
Marie-Sophie Schwarzer

**Images**
Roos Aldershoff
Annelore Photography
Benthem Crouwel Architects
Arjan Bronkhorst
Christiaan de Bruijne
Ellen de Bruijne Projects
Fred Ernst
Luuk Kramer
John Lewis Marshall
Jannes Linders
Matteo Rossi
Ruud Splinter
Rob 't Hart
Marcel van der Burg
Ton van Namen
Gert Jan van Rooi

**Illustrators**
Satoshi Hashimoto
Ceylan Sahin Eker
Tokuma

**Monocle**
EDITOR IN CHIEF AND CHAIRMAN
*Tyler Brûlé*
EDITOR
*Andrew Tuck*
CREATIVE DIRECTOR
*Richard Spencer Powell*

CHAPTER EDITING

**Need to know**
*Mikaela Aitken*
*Pauline den Hartog Jager*

**Hotels**
*Mikaela Aitken*

**Food and drink**
*Venetia Rainey*

**Retail**
*Nolan Giles*

**Things we'd buy**
*Mikaela Aitken*
*Nolan Giles*

**Essays**
*Mikaela Aitken*
*Pauline den Hartog Jager*

**Culture**
*Mikaela Aitken*

**Design and architecture**
*Mikaela Aitken*

**Sport and fitness**
*Mikaela Aitken*

**Walks**
*Mikaela Aitken*

**Resources**
*Venetia Rainey*


**The Monocle Travel Guide
Series: Amsterdam**
GUIDE EDITOR
*Mikaela Aitken*
ASSOCIATE GUIDE EDITORS
*Nolan Giles*
*Joleen Goffin*
PHOTO EDITOR
*Victoria Cagol*

**The Monocle Travel Guide
Series**
SERIES EDITOR
*Joe Pickard*
ASSOCIATE EDITOR
*Chloë Ashby*
ASSISTANT EDITOR
*Mikaela Aitken*
RESEARCHER
*Melkon Charchoglyan*
DESIGNERS
*Loi Xuan Ly*
*Jay Yeo*
PHOTO EDITORS
*Matthew Beaman*
*Victoria Cagol*
*Shin Miura*

PRODUCTION
*Jacqueline Deacon*
*Dan Poole*
*Rachel Kurzfield*
*Sean McGeady*
*Sonia Zhuravlyova*


**Research**
*Melkon Charchoglyan*
*Tom Furse*
*Naomi Joseph*
*Ian Keddie*
*Charles McFarlane*
*Aliz Tennant*
*Ceinwen Thomas*

**Special thanks**
*Arcam*
*Kathy Ball*
*Yoko Choy*
*Sabine de Witte*
*Yana Foqué*
*Aron Friedman*
*High45*
*I Amsterdam*
*Pete Kempshall*
*Rhiannon Pickles*
*Amy Richardson*
*Sanne Visser*
*Shanthi Voorn*
*X Bank*

**New**

*The MONOCLE Travel Guide Series* **20** Ⓜ
# Venice

*... Ooh! Glide through the laguna city's outposts of good food, design, retail and more. Andiamo! ...*

*The MONOCLE Travel Guide Series* **22** Ⓜ
# Stockholm

*... Hej! Wander with us through the city's outposts of good food, design, retail and more. Trevlig resa! ...*

Ⓜ
**Buy today at all good bookshops**

You can also visit the online shops at *monocle.com* and *shop.gestalten.com* to get hold of your copies

## The collection

We hope you have found the Monocle Travel Guide to Amsterdam useful, inspiring and entertaining. There's plenty more to get your teeth into: we have a global suite of guides, with many more set to be released in the coming months. Cities are fun. Let's explore.

### ❶ London
The sights, sounds and style

### ❷ New York
Get a taste of the Big Apple's best

### ❸ Tokyo
The enigmatic glory of Japan's capital

### ❹ Hong Kong
Down to business in this vibrant city

### ❺ Madrid
Captivating capital abuzz with spirit

### ❻ Bangkok
Stimulate your senses with the exotic

### ❼ Istanbul
Thrilling fusion of Asia and Europe

### ❽ Miami
Unpack the Magic City's box of tricks

### ❾ Rio de Janeiro
Beaches, bars and bossa nova

### ❿ Paris
Be romanced by the City of Light

### ⓫ Singapore
Where modernity meets tradition

### ⓬ Vienna
Waltz through the Austrian capital

### ⓭ Sydney
Sun, surf and urban delights

### ⓮ Honolulu
Embrace Hawaii's aloha spirit

### ⓯ Copenhagen
Cycle through the Danish capital

### ⓰ Los Angeles
Fly high in the City of Angels

### ⓱ Toronto
Delve into this diverse Canadian city

### ⓲ Berlin
Discover the city of two halves

### ⓳ Rome
Scoot through the Eternal City

### ⓴ Venice
Wonder at the waterways

### ㉑ Amsterdam
Canals, bicycles and liberalism

*So, where to next?*